The Journey Home

40 Days of Thoughts, Prayers and Encouragement from the Celts

STEVE MORRIS

Authentic

First published 2020 by Authentic Media Limited,
PO Box 6326, Bletchley, Milton Keynes,
MK1 9GG.
authenticmedia.co.uk

British Library Cataloguing in Publication Data
A catalogue record for this book is available from the British Library.
ISBN: 978-1-78893-195-3
978-1-78893-192-2 (e-book)

Royalties from the sale of this book will go to the
Motor Neurone Disease Association.
MND Association: Registered in England.
Registered Charity no. 294354.
Registered office: Francis Crick House, Summerhouse Road, Moulton
Park Industrial Estate, Northampton, England, NN3 6BF.

Cover design by Arnel Gregorio
of Arrow Designs
Arrowdesigns01@gmail.com

Contents

Foreword

Prayer and life were not two separate entities to the Celtic Christians, our ancestors in the faith. They would never dream that prayer was for high days and holy days only or that they could only be said in certain holy places. Prayer encompassed their lives from waking in the morning until closing their eyes for sleep at night. Everything was soaked in prayer, for God was both all-powerful and Lord of all creation, yet at the same time closer to us than our own breath. They had a vivid sense of God's presence everywhere. For these pre-industrial Christians, the important things in life were keeping warm and having food on the table, but they also valued relationships: family and friends featured in their petitions for safety and protection from danger. They brought their needs to God, but in their prayers they also expressed what they believed about God. They had come to know that he was the 'maker of all things', the Lord and giver of life and that he loved the world so much that he came and lived among us, dying for us and rising again. God, by his Spirit, was everywhere and nothing was beyond his loving concern. Knowing God in this way gave their lives meaning and instilled in them a joy and gratitude that spills over into their praying. They spread this good news around these islands and laid the foundations of the faith that we have inherited in our own time. The streams of living water that were embodied in these early saints lived on so that when Alexander Carmichael traversed the Highlands as a customs and excise officer in the nineteenth century he heard prayers and poems that echoed the same rhythms and cadences of those who first brought Christ to that area.

Our lives may look very different, but we share the same concerns: our need for the basic necessities, for food and safety and friendship.

Many older people were taught to memorize prayers such as the weekly collect from the Book of Common Prayer. Today few young people know any prayers beyond perhaps the Lord's Prayer. To have a store of prayers in our memory is to carry around with us a treasure house of spiritual nourishment. Celtic prayers stay in the mind. They are memorable because of their rhythm, and the frequent repetition not only aids us in memorizing them but teaches us important truths about God and the world. They also remind us of the vital importance of being connected to the natural world, which is more significant at this time in our history than ever before. Never sentimental in their relationship with nature, the Celtic Christians valued it and rejoiced in the sheer wonder of it, for they saw in it reflections of the character of its Creator. We have lost our sense of interconnectedness with one another and with the natural world to our great cost, and our lives are the poorer for it. As we teeter on the brink of the consequences of our terrible neglect and exploitation of the natural environment, praying with the Celts is one way of realizing its importance, and prayer is the first step towards transformed ways of living in the light of God's purposes for us.

By offering a prayer for each day with a reflection on its meaning and use, Steve is giving us an aid to help us enrich prayer in our daily lives. His contemporary prayer reminds us that ancient prayers can be a springboard for our prayers. We may not be poets but we can express our needs and longings to God direct from our hearts in simple words of our own. They also remind us to be thankful for the ordinary but vital things that give us life and help us to be joyful and hopeful, even in the midst of difficulties. Many of the prayers were offered online during the recent coronavirus pandemic. They had special relevance for people facing an unknown and uncontrollable threat, often isolated and alone. Life for Christians in an earlier age was no less threatening. They too had to deal with fear, a future that was unknown and the threat of losing hope. Hostile enemies, plague and adverse weather were just a few things that could paralyse people and lead them to question faith in a loving God. These prayers speak otherwise, however, expressing hope and even joy in the face of adversity.

Liz Hoare
Wycliffe Hall, Oxford

Acknowledgements

Thank you to the team at my publisher, Authentic. They have put up with me with remarkable good heart and patience. Thank you, too, to my friends at *The Oldie*, the *Church of England Newspaper* and *The Spectator* who have seen the value in these ancient prayers. I am indebted to Michael Mitton and the folk at Scargill House for an excellent week away studying and immersing ourselves in the world of the Celtic Christians. Thank you, too, to Tina Last who read the manuscript and helped to smooth it out.

I have been accompanied on the journey of this book by my family, who have been patient, and by my three cats, Lance, Luna and Megan. The cats have joined me on many occasions and encouraged me with their purring and their kindly ways. They have also added various letters to the manuscript by walking on the keyboard. I wish cats could spell because, if they could, I would have left their contributions in.

*I arise today, through
God's strength to pilot me,
God's might to uphold me,
God's wisdom to guide me,
God's eye to look before me,
God's ear to hear me,
God's word to speak for me,
God's hand to guard me,
God's shield to protect me,
God's host to save me
From snares of devils,
From temptation of vices,
From everyone who shall wish me ill,
afar and near.*

'St Patrick's Breastplate'

Getting Started

Hope in the Face of Peril

I write this from my vicarage in north London. I'm just a few minutes away from Northwick Park Hospital, which is one of the centres of excellence for treating people with the Covid-19 virus. It is a sobering time. Every few minutes, an ambulance speeds past, sirens blaring – and in each of those ambulances is a precious person, perhaps fighting for their life. Maybe we all wonder whether we will ever be safe again. We are certainly going to see great changes in our society as a result. Life will never be quite the same again.

We have been robbed, for the time being, of that which makes us so special – the close company of people we love. Having dropped off food to my dear mum, it was heartbreaking to just be able to wave at each other through the window. It seemed very cruel.

When I got home, she rang me. 'Steven, I will be really annoyed if I die in the end from this virus, when I've spent all this time indoors.' The human spirit and a touch of humour can never be squashed it seems.

It can seem difficult to know what to pray and how to pray. I have found myself turning to some of the ancient prayers of our forebears, and I have found these very comforting. In many ways, discovering the spirituality and struggles from all those centuries ago has helped me to know that one day this will be over. We are not the first generation to face seismic change and a sense of dislocation. Indeed, history teaches us that we have been fortunate to avoid major upheavals for many decades.

I came to faith in a charismatic church where we tended to extemporize our prayers. I still enjoy that way of praying and in no way look down upon it. The freedom of charismatic prayers can be exhilarating and often gives a strong sense of the work of the Holy Spirit.

However, in recent years I've begun to enjoy the ancient prayers that have been prayed through the centuries. It is a relief not to have to invent new prayers and simply to pray along with all of those who have prayed them before. Rather than this being stale, it has reinvigorated my prayer life and helped me appreciate that our generation stands on the shoulders of spiritual giants from previous generations. The ancient prayers have power and they bring us comfort. In times when I feel flat and can't come up with the words of a prayer, I am able to join in with the prayers that have been prayed before.

There is an ancient Celtic prayer that is as relevant today as it was all those centuries ago.

> *Be Thou a smooth way before me,*
> *Be Thou a guiding star above me,*
> *Be Thou a keen eye behind me,*
> *This day, this night, for ever.*
> *I am weary, and I am forlorn,*
> *Lead Thou me to the land of the angels;*
> *Methinks it were time I went for a space*
> *To the court of Christ, to the peace of heaven.*
>
> *Carmina Gadelica*, Prayer 266[1]

It sets the tone for so much of the ancient poetry and prayers. It acknowledges that life can be difficult and plain scary, and we can feel weary. We sometimes need a break! I am sure this speaks directly into the situation of many – those in small flats trying to reassure and look after children for instance. It is also beautifully honest and psychologically true.

Normally, we experience life as a settled pattern where today is very much like yesterday and we can be pretty sure that tomorrow will be like today. As a modern person, I rarely think about my own mortality. I have a sense that modern medicine, the rule of law and order and general good luck should keep me safe.

With the daily fear of death removed, we have been free to think about other things. But this crisis has driven us back to the primeval past, to a sense of fellowship with our ancient forebears who knew only too well that there were things perilous and that there are things that feel dark and oppressive. In this little jewel of a prayer poem, we get both a reality check and a sense of danger which we probably are all feeling now. Indeed, we get a dissection of the business of weariness, low spirits and anxiety. Having read it, I realized that we're not the only generation to feel that.

But there is one thing that shines through in this prayer. It is the urgent desire of the person who spoke it to invoke, to summon and to pray for the presence of God who will stand between us and all that makes for this kind of existential darkness and despair. If God has got our back and is making smooth the path, then we have a fighting chance of remaining hopeful.

Perhaps one of our deepest desires is to feel safe and to feel at home. Underlying the whole narrative of the Bible is that sense of homecoming and safety. In the Old Testament the Israelites, after forty years in the wilderness, make it home. It must have been quite a relief. Of course, in the New Testament we realize that home is where God is: the person of Christ made available to all of us to care for us, walk with us and love us. The ancient Celtic prayers have a strong sense of home. Indeed, they are intrinsically homely and paint a picture of a God who is, yes, mighty, but is also domestic and close to us and kindly. In these times when we worry about how we will ever return to normality and how our loved ones will fare, this domesticity and comfort is most welcome. In this short book I aim to provide comfort and prayers and a sense of normality, which it seems to me, at least, are most needed.

In these strange times it might do us good to hear the comforting songs, prayers and poems of the people who understood the value of community and feasting and singing and the joy of the creation and all the things that make us feel as though we are alive. The Celtic Christians had an inherent optimism which is infectious.

A Resource for the Coming Months and Years

While this book has been written at a time and place, I hope that it will be a great comfort throughout the coming months and years. This pandemic will be over, and life will return to something like normal. The greatest minds on the planet are working on finding cures and helping us to get through this terrible time.

I certainly hope that at the end of it we will be a much more collegiate society and much more appreciative of those who bring to us the means by which we survive and thrive. So, while I've written it during lockdown it is for much more than just this. I hope that once kindled, the love of the ancient prayers will sustain you throughout your Christian journey. They might open a doorway for seeing the God of love and gentleness afresh.

I have been a writer for many years. You might say that I am in love with language and the way that words work. These little Celtic beauties bring out the very best in our language and make a deep dent in our hearts at the same time. I hope that my enthusiasm for them overcomes any other weaknesses in my commentary on the verses. I encourage you to spend time with the Celtic Christians and with the prayers and poems that seem to speak so directly to us in our world today.

I make sure that I read one Celtic poem or prayer every day because they make me feel good and help to build my faith. I have started a Celtic service once a month here, where we enjoy listening to the Celtic prayers and keeping some silence. People tell me that these services give them a chance to relax and be themselves. It is an interesting observation and an unintended critique of what we do the rest of the time in church, perhaps. They are certainly a pleasure to lead.

Our Celtic Roots

Celtic Christianity started after the Romans left Britain in 410. In 635 an Irish monk, St Columba, came to Iona and set up a church and monastic community. He converted pagans in Scotland and northern England, and over the centuries these monasteries became centres of creativity, learning and enterprise.

Day-to-day life was very uncertain. There was plague and smallpox which ravaged everyday life and touched everyone, including some of the great saints who probably died of disease. It was a time when the population decreased partly because of poverty, partly because of wars. And then, of course, there was the problem of illness. If that wasn't enough, there was also the issue of invasion by the Vikings.

Everyone living in Celtic Britain understood that life was inherently risky, under threat, and, by extension, precious. They tended to pull together and to work together. Family was important.

We have these extraordinary prayers courtesy of a Victorian ethnographer and tax collector called Alexander Carmichael. He worked in the Hebrides and Scottish Highlands and wrote the prayers and blessings and stories down as he visited working people in the course of his labours. He realized that he was hearing voices handed down through the generations; that, while listening to people, he was also hearing the voices of their ancestors. Remember, learning things by heart and then retelling them was a crucial element before people could read and write or there was widespread access to writing materials. Perhaps they could rely on their memories more than we can. The book Carmichael compiled is called *Carmina Gadelica* and is a treasure-trove of hundreds of poems and stories.

The other great resource is Alistair Maclean's beautiful book of Celtic reminiscences, poems and stories, *Hebridean Altars*. He followed in the footsteps of Alexander Carmichael and he too was fascinated by the stories he heard in the Hebrides. His book, published in 1937, has over one hundred prayers, poems and sayings from the Christian tradition of the author's native Hebrides.

The Celtic prayers never ducked the difficulties of life but managed to remain hopeful in the face of the great contingency of being alive. They're full of homely detail and great gratitude for what they find around them. They are rooted in nature and in community.

Being in lockdown, I have frequently taken to sitting in my vicarage garden. I'm no great gardener, and I'm more likely to kill a plant than to grow it. But, with the traffic noise having gone from the road outside and without planes landing at Heathrow Airport, there is one sound that has been a huge comfort to me over these last weeks.

Each day, I have been able to listen to the birds and marvel at their glorious songs, and this has given me a tremendous sense of hope. The great Celtic saints struck up friendships with animals both wild and domestic. St Cuthbert was rescued from starvation by a wild eagle who shared a salmon with him, and he struck up a friendship with the sea otters who would dry and warm his legs after he had been in the cold sea praying to God. Animals were cherished as were the trees and plants. If you live off the land and on the land, then it becomes more of a friend and ally than something to be exploited to the hilt.

Watching as spring begins, I'm realizing that nothing can stop the flowers growing and the birds singing, and this has given me a great sense that one day this will be over. The Celts believed that this earth is our home and that it is intrinsically good because it shows God's goodness and creativity. It is a gift to us.

And so, this short book is an offering. It is for us over the next few months, and perhaps years, as we deal with a world that seems much less certain and much riskier.

Rather as a fine meal should never disguise the unique taste of the ingredients, it is important we let these ancient prayers speak for themselves and don't get in the way too much. I hope and pray that I leave enough room for them to speak down through the ages as they have done to me.

The book covers the period of forty days because that is the period Christ spent in the wilderness. Forty is something of a magic number in biblical terms. While Jesus was in the wilderness, he was tempted to despair. He must have felt very lonely and vulnerable. It's interesting that he was also buoyed up by the wild creatures in that wilderness. He didn't eat them. Instead he enjoyed their company and they helped him get through a very difficult experience indeed. The Celtic Christians also felt a great affinity with the animals around them – even the wild and dangerous ones.

A Word of Warning

I write this book not as an academic expert on Celtic spirituality. I have become interested in it through my experiences of running a Celtic service at my own church and knowing that the Celtic Way has helped to guide me on my own spiritual path. Any inaccuracies or errors are entirely my fault.

Steve Morris
St Cuthbert's, North Wembley, Easter Day 2020

PART ONE

Feeling Anxious
and Unsure

Day 1

Bewildered and Scared

I am bewildered by so many things. I asked myself why the little one is taken from the mother's breast: why the bonds of married life are severed ere even love's noon is come: or the dreams Thou has sent us reach not the haven of fulfilment. Jesus, Thou Light of men bring me out of my groping into the radiance of Thy truth. Yet if Thou withholdest Thy light from me because my eyes cannot bear its brightness, still give me what is needful to make my dark be gone.

Hebridean Altars[2]

Where better to start than where most of us are currently at? It seems like only yesterday the things we took for granted were all around us. Just four weeks ago, my family and I had headed out for breakfast on Saturday morning and then over to the bookshop to browse and to enjoy a cup of coffee. Everything has changed – at least for now.

I am fifty-seven and come from the blessed generation that never really had to fight a war and didn't undergo too many privations. Yes, there were power cuts and disturbances in the 1970s. Yes, there have been times when our nation has seemed more stable than others. And I do remember a constant fear when growing up of nuclear conflict. However, compared to almost every other generation in the history of Great Britain, this has been an unprecedented time of feeling settled. It was as though we were immune to global disaster.

I don't think any of us could have imagined just a short time ago that we might feel frightened of going out or touching the envelope that had just been delivered by the postal worker.

The first stage in any rehabilitation is to acknowledge the way that we are feeling. We tend to think that we are more open about our feelings than previous generations, but look at this extraordinary gem of a Celtic prayer written probably sometime just after the fifth century and hear the ring of emotional truth that is deep within it.

The concerns are extraordinarily contemporary. This ancient prayer begins with: 'I am bewildered by so many things.' Aren't we all? The author has a sense of bafflement about the business of life and why there is so much injustice and suffering. This doesn't spill over into direct anger at God, instead it leads to questions.

I have always loved the word 'bewilderment'. It is one of those old words, with a touch of mystery about it. Its root is in being lost in the wilderness. In our modern world there are few wildernesses left. But we seem to be in one now in this time of anxiety and uncertainty. It is an internal wilderness.

The fragility of love and marriage is a great mystery and a great sadness. The author acknowledges this. Why do we dream of things when our dreams can be so easily snatched away? Was failure, ruin and the ending of our hopes part of God's plan? Of course not, but where does that leave us?

The prayer performs a twist that is a great comfort to us. The author acknowledges that Christ *is* the light of men and women and that only in that light might we be able to discern some of the answers to the big questions of life. Of course, these are the questions many of us are asking now.

There are many kinds of darkness in each of our lives. I'm finding that during this lockdown I'm having some good days and some bad days and I'm sure I'm not alone in this. I do want to join, though, in this prayer that *my* darkness, and the darkness of my friends and all those around me, will be gone. As the author says: 'Give me what is needful to make my dark be gone.' Reassurance, peace, courage, patience and fortitude would all seem to be on that list.

My prayer

*Dear Father, I'm often bewildered and unsure.
When the world seems a confusing and dangerous
place, I don't always know where to turn. I need
the resources to know what to do next and how
best to proceed. Would you reassure me and give
me courage for the journey ahead? I don't need to
know everything and to cover every risk, but just
enough to help bring light into my life and the life
of those around me. Amen*

Day 2

The Giant Thumb

I lie in my bed
As I would lie in the grave,
Thine arm beneath my neck,
Thou son of Mary victorious.

Angels shall watch me
And I lying in slumber,
And angels shall guard me
In the sleep of the grave.

Carmina Gadelica, Prayer 40[3]

I once had a friend who described to me the feeling of being under spiritual attack. Not attack by physical forces or other people, but by that strange sense of psychological oppression that many of us feel from time to time. We have medical terms to describe this sense when it cripples us – we call it anxiety.

On Sundays, as a boy, I would always begin to start feeling that sense of anxiety. I suppose it was because I was worried about going to school the next day. I remember that on Sunday evenings I loved it when my family would play board games or just sit together and watch telly because it would help me feel just a bit more normal and less anxious about the day that was to come. We all sometimes feel a deep disquiet.

In these times we dread, don't we, the sense of what might be coming our way? My friend described this feeling as 'the giant thumb'. He said that there were times when he felt as though a giant thumb was pressing down upon him and that he was being squashed by it. I've always felt that this is one of the best descriptions I've ever heard of a sense of oppression, of anxiety and a sense of dread.

Oppression can come from our daily lives and the circumstances we face. But it can also come from supernatural forces. If we accept that there is an eternal battle in the heavens between the forces of good and bad, then we might need to accept that sometimes we experience some ripples of that.

It's odd that we so often feel this way when we're about to go to sleep. We may be sophisticated and scientifically aware people, but we still have an ancient fear of the dark and what it might bring. I wonder if it is a defence mechanism, but I do know that we all wonder sometimes how the night is going to be. It doesn't help that during these intense times, people have reported having vivid and terrifying dreams. These are the old-fashioned terrors of the night that we are contending with.

This Celtic prayer is a masterpiece. In just a few words it manages to sum up what it feels like to have that giant thumb pushing down on us. The author understands that sometimes when we lie down in bed we can feel as though it is a kind of grave. It is a very strong image.

What I so love about the Celtic prayers and poems is that sense of mystery and ambiguity about them. They don't go for the easy formulas. In this prayer poem, the writer feels as though their bed is a grave and wants Christ's arm as a pillow. It is a touching image – as though Christ is lying right next to us and, simply reaching over, puts his arm under our neck and relieves some of the pressure we are feeling. It is the most natural act of reassurance imaginable.

Some people have a squeamishness about the ministry of angels. They worry that they are sometimes a substitute for the saving power of Christ. But it is telling that Christ calls upon the help of the angels to give him enough hope and fortitude to get to the cross. I often think that if Christ was able to enjoy the ministry of angels, then why can't we do just the same thing?

The thought that, while we sleep and when we feel anxious, angels are at our bedside guiding us and whispering words of comfort to us is very reassuring and is something that many of us hope for. I like to repeat these words from the prayer.

Angels shall watch me
And I lying in slumber,
And angels shall guard me
In the sleep of the grave.

The Celtic Christians had a strong sense of the ministry of angels. They felt their presence in everyday life. In these troubled times, I can see no problem with asking the Lord to send an angel or two to guard us and our families.

My prayer

Dear Father, please send your mighty angels to protect me and those whom I love this evening. Send them to guard my bed and my house. Help me to sleep soundly and without troubling dreams. When I feel fearful, reassure me and fill me full of the joy and peace of your Holy Spirit. Amen

---

Day 3

Love Conquers Fear

When mystery hides Thee from the sight of faith and hope: when pain turns even love to dust: when life is bitter to the taste and our song of joy dies down to silence, then, Father, do for us that which is past our power to do for ourselves. Break through our darkness with Thy light. Show us Thyself in Jesus suffering on a Tree, rising from a grave, reigning from a throne, all with power and love for us unchanging. So shall our fear be gone, and our feet set upon a radiant path.

Hebridean Altars[4]

It always strikes me as deeply profound that the opposite of love is not hate, but fear. Fear is a potent force. Sometimes fear is a good thing, of course. We are hard-wired for fight or flight and when we face real danger, we sometimes feel we need to make a choice between the two.

This ancient paragraph dissects our feelings of hopelessness and fear; it is a clinical description. There's a sense that sometimes life is so mysterious that we lose sight of our faith and sometimes our hope dries up as well. As the author knows, love can become dust, life can become bitter and our song of joy can be choked before it leaves our lips. We have modern words to describe this condition and we call it depression. There are days when the 'black dog', as Winston Churchill called it, will not leave us alone and we wonder whether we'll ever be normal again.

This beautiful prayer is an exceptionally mature understanding of what it is to be a person of faith in difficult and gloomy times. When we can't see our families and we are concerned about their wellbeing and we wonder how our world will ever be put together again, it wouldn't be surprising if our song of joy became silence in the face of such uncertainty and suffering.

So, what do we do with this? Is it a cul-de-sac or path to something better? What do we do with these uncomfortable feelings and perceptions that we are all living with? The first thing to do is to acknowledge the darkness. It's all very good to have the blitz spirit and to be cheerful – why not? But at some point, we need to accept, voice and inhabit the fact that this is an extremely difficult time. When we have that in the open, we can move on to somewhere else. Acknowledgement is the first stage of recovery.

This poem asks us to actively pray for breakthrough – not just to accept our lot. It is an active faith at work here. It acknowledges that the only way of piercing the darkness is with God's light, and the author asks Jesus to show himself. Interestingly, this isn't a call at first for the radiant Jesus of triumph and lordship. No, our comfort, our resilience comes from joining Jesus as he suffers on the cross. The cross is a pivotal moment of human history, but it doesn't end there, as the writer understands. After the cross, came rising from the grave, the ascension.

We feel fearful; we are children in adults' bodies, and we do not like it when we don't know the future. But this beautiful prayer poem paints an image that is helpful. In the great scope of Christ's ministry – from birth, life, death, resurrection and ascension into glory – our fear can be diminished because we set our feet upon the same radiant path as he did. Being a bit fearful is not a sign of poor faith, though. It is part of the human condition. Jesus himself felt fear and anxiety and sadness. Of course, how would we follow him if he had not shared in our humanity? But this little beauty helps me to keep the fear at bay even if just for a short while.

Break through our darkness with Thy light. Show us Thyself in Jesus suffering on a Tree, rising from a grave, reigning from a throne, all with power and love for us unchanging. So shall our fear be gone, and our feet set upon a radiant path.

My prayer

*Dear Father, love conquers fear and sometimes
I am very fearful. I know that in you there is no
darkness and when I think about the power of your
love I begin to feel better and more peaceful. Show
me the path ahead lit with glorious lights, that I
might walk upon it straight into the heart of your
love for us. Amen*

Day 4

From Restlessness and Fear to Peace

Alexander Carmichael adds an intriguing note as he transcribes the following prayer. This prayer of protection came from a meeting with a lonely, old and very poor woman who he met one day while working in the Hebrides. She shared with him something of her faith and practice of her faith and the rituals she had. One of these was making the sign of the cross on her pillow before she slept. After making the sign she would pray:

May the light of lights come
To my dark heart from Thy place;
May the Spirit's wisdom come
To my heart's tablet from my Saviour.

Be the peace of the Spirit mine this night,
Be the peace of the Son mine this night,
Be the peace of the Father mine this night,
The peace of all peace be mine this night,
Each morning and evening of my life.

Carmina Gadelica Prayer 239[5]

It would be easy to write off the practice of making the sign of a cross on the pillow as a kind of superstition. But I see it more as evidence of the importance of symbols in the faith; sometimes simply making a sign of the cross reassures us and we get a great sense of God.

Carmichael was in a somewhat difficult position. It's hard to imagine that he was the most popular caller that these poor folks had to deal with. But over the years, he won their trust, probably because he became skilled at listening. I have long thought that the art of listening to other people's stories is at the heart of the faith. Indeed, my book, *Our Precious Lives*, is all about that. If we are truly to acknowledge the incarnation, that everyday life is holy and that our lives are holy, then we do well to honour the lives around us.

I like this poem prayer because it acknowledges we sometimes feel the greatest darkness that comes from within. Sometimes darkness has been with us for many years and we wonder how we might shake it off. In these times, it's easy to lose perspective, but this ancient prayer seems to say that if we can listen to the ministering of the Holy Spirit, then we might be able to get things into perspective. I like it that the prayer goes from an acknowledgement of darkness and the ups and downs of the human heart and lands on a very simple and direct request. The author has a need for a feeling of peace. Don't we all?

I have long thought that peace is one of those rare commodities in our modern world and it's tempting to look back on the distant past and paint it as a rural idyll. In fact, it was hard, and life was tough and sometimes brutal.

In *these* brutal times as well, we all yearn for peace. At least I do.

My prayer

*Dear Father, I am sometimes fretful and restless.
I cannot settle and I cannot concentrate.
Throughout my life I have yearned for peace and a
sense of being safe and at home. Would you calm
me down and help me to know that all shall be
well. Many people, I know, are also restless, help
us all to settle into your gentle love. Amen*

PART TWO

We Need Protecting

Day 5

Better than a Horseshoe

God, bless the world and all that is therein.
God, bless my spouse and my children,
God, bless the eye that is in my head,
And bless, O God, the handling of my hand;
What time I rise in the morning early,
What time I lie down late in bed . . .
God, protect the house, and the household,
God, consecrate the children of the motherhood,
God, encompass the flocks and the young;
Be thou after them and tending them,
What time the flocks ascend hill and wold,
What time I lie down in peace to sleep . . .

Carmina Gadelica, Prayer 44[6]

I grew up in Northolt, right on the far edge of west London. We lived in a small house and my parents paid a great deal of attention to it. This was the first house my father had ever owned – his family for generations before would have rented.

Nailed to the wall in the back garden was an upside-down horseshoe. My father was an old East Ender and, like many from that part of London, he was quite superstitious. He saw the horseshoe as something of a good-luck charm, a way of keeping us all safe in the house. Good fortune would be trapped in the horseshoe and kept there as a kind of charm.

I suppose it's understandable that he worried about safety. He was bombed out twice during the Second World War. The first time was when he was in Canning Town in the east end of London. The next time came, I think, when they had relocated to Finchley. Many people were killed and my father, his sister and his mother just about survived, but their house was blown to pieces. He remembered the terrible sound when the bomb hit the house, and the moment, when the dust had literally settled, that the family, huddled under the kitchen table, saw that everything else was rubble. They lost everything, and my father had dreams of that moment for the rest of his life. I am in awe of the way the family managed to pull together.

Our Celtic forebears didn't need to deal with incendiary bombs or modern machines of destruction. However, they did know what it was like to not sleep safely in their beds. There were constant worries. In many ways, life then was like an episode of *Game of Thrones* with warring households and factions spilling a great deal of blood; people felt vulnerable. As a parent I always feel it is my primary responsibility to keep my family safe.

This prayer manages to encompass so many different things. It begins on a grand scale by asking God to bless the world and it then moves down to a more domestic level with the desire for spouse and children to be blessed. It asks for blessing throughout the day. They would, of course, have got up at dawn while many of us these days are still sleeping when the birds begin singing. The call for blessing is for it to be constant and to cover all of life.

The close cousin of blessing is protecting. I think we've all felt the need for a protector. This simple yet beautiful prayer encompasses everything that the speaker loves and cares about under the great wing of God's protection. There is the house and the household; the children and their mother, and there is more. Families relied upon their livestock – they cared for them and they saw it as a godly duty to protect them. This prayer brings into the fold the flocks and the young animals and those who tend them: the shepherds. It paints a picture of the domestic life of these people and asks God to protect the whole lot of it.

Sometimes when I lie down to sleep here in the vicarage, I feel troubled and I pray a father's prayer for the protection of my children and my wife and my cats and for those I love so very much. I stand alongside the Celtic Christians who did the same thing.

My prayer

Dear Father, we all know the need for your protection. Sometimes we are too shy to ask for it. But we need it now and we ask you to protect our homes and the people we care for.
Amen

Day 6

Standing under the Protection
of the Cross

Christ's cross over this face, and thus over my ear.
Christ's cross over this eye.
Christ's cross over this nose.
Christ's cross before me to accompany me.
Christ's cross behind me to accompany me.
Christ's cross to meet every difficulty both on hollow and hill.
Christ's cross eastwards facing me.
Christ's cross back towards the sunset.
In the north, in the south, increasingly may Christ's cross straightway be.
Christ's cross up to broad Heaven.
Christ's cross down to earth.
Let no evil or hurt come to my body or my soul.
Christ's cross over me as I sit.
Christ's cross over me as I lie.
Christ's cross be all my strength until we reach the King of Heaven.
From the top of my head to the nail of my toe, O Christ, against every danger I trust in the protection of the cross.

*Till the day of my death, going into the clay, I shall draw with-
out – Christ's cross over this face.*

Ninth-century Irish, author unknown

How far does the protection of the cross stretch? The crucifixion of
the God who made the universe and loves each and every one of us is
a fact. There are some very interesting books that subject the evidence
of the cross to legal examination and certainly on the balance of all
probability it looks as though it happened as it said it happened.

But there is more to the cross than simply being the site of one of
the most atrocious crimes imaginable. The cross also speaks of God
protecting us and the cloak of care that Christ's self-giving action was
part of.

In this ninth-century Celtic prayer, we see the cross stretching its influence far and wide. Christ's cross covers the face, the body and the earth.
Christ's cross reminds us of his protection when we sit and when we
sleep; it reminds us that in every danger we can rely upon the protection
of the cross.

The action of God upon the cross vouches for his deep care for us and
his promise to stand with us in all our sufferings. For me the cross isn't
so much a symbol or a talisman – it is the deepest truth that under-
pins the world. The truth of the cross – that love wins – is a protection
against cynicism, despair and evil. It is mighty – or at least, Jesus is
mighty and his agony, his passion, speak of the winning of the war
against all that is bad in this world. The big battle has been won; we
are still involved in skirmishes.

If we were to look with the eyes of our heart, we might see the cross
still standing, but empty of the Christ. It is the vista that asserts that
evil and violence will never win and perhaps that is the greatest protection and hope we have.

_____

My prayer

Dear Father, we stand under the protection of the cross. The cross stands above us and its shadow falls upon us as well. We are thankful for the love of Jesus. Thank you that the cross shows us that love wins and we pray for your reassurance this very evening that we have the covering of the cross to keep us safe. Amen

_____

Day 7

Protection on a Cheerless Day

Though the dawn breaks cheerless on this Isle today, my spirit walks upon a path of light. For I know my greatness. Thou hast built me a throne within Thy heart. I dwell safely within the circle of Thy care. I cannot for a moment fall out of Thine everlasting arms. I am on my way to Thy glory.

Hebridean Altars[7]

This prayer poem seems to suggest that it can be a bit grim up north. I'm certainly very much affected by the weather. Over the years, I have specialized in going on holiday on the only week in which it rains in that particular place. I sometimes think that I should be invited to places that are short of water because my appearance on holiday, complete with suitcase and swimming costume, is bound to bring a deluge of biblical proportions. I certainly find that by the time it gets to about January I am really worn down by the grey days, the rain and the lack of sunshine. I sometimes wish I lived in a hot country, so I could get, not just vitamin D, but also that sunshine boost that we all need.

All of us have known cheerless starts to the day. It is truly horrible when we get out of bed and we have the thought that the day isn't going to improve very much. This prayer begins with that sense of greyness but asserts that God's protection can transcend even the most cheerless circumstances. Sometimes our joy is completely sucked out of us, and over the past few weeks it's been very hard to keep up the sunny face for a long time. Yes, we know that one day this will be over and that the finest minds are working on solutions, but we miss so much so many things about life as it was just a few weeks ago.

In this prayer even though the dawn is cheerless, the person who spoke it takes heart that their spirit is walking on a path of light. It is a lovely image – like a runway at night lit by landing lights and keeping everyone safe. It is also the inner assurance that they are loved by God and that somehow God has set up shop inside that person's heart that gives them a sense of security. They know that with God with them they are within the great circle of his care.

When I was young, I fell into a swimming pool while on holiday. I banged my head badly and I became disorientated. Thankfully, my father had spotted what was going on and he rushed over to the side of the pool, jumped in, lifted me up and grabbed hold of me. I gave him the most terrible scare. He held on to me tightly. I was grateful at the time, but I think I didn't really understand the depth of that experience. Now that I am a parent, I know just how precious my children are and how I would do anything to rescue them if they need help. I will always be there.

> *I cannot for a moment fall out of Thine everlasting arms. I am on my way to Thy glory.*

There is a beautiful image in this poem prayer. It talks about us being in God's care and that we cannot for a moment fall out of his everlasting arms. Everlasting arms doesn't mean great long arms, it just means that God promises to hold us tight. We are in God's embrace and we can feel protected because we are on the road to glory, where we will never be separated from each other again.

Another way of seeing this is that we are all on the road home. One day, regardless of how this life has treated us, we will be heading home to a place without tears and suffering. Bad things happen in life, we all know that. We cannot insulate ourselves against the ups and downs of life or sheer bad luck. We might be in the wrong place at the wrong time. These trying times have reminded us how fragile life can be.

Yes, we pray for protection, we pray to come through this unscathed as well as all our loved ones and everyone else. But God's protection extends into eternity. It is the protection that says all shall be well. It gives me great comfort to think that I, and those around me, are on the path of light, even if it seems that we are lost on a boggy track without a map at times.

We will look later at some classic Celtic prayer poems about pilgrimage and journeys. Celtic Christians understood that we are always on the move in some way, but that God is the one who promises to accompany us. We are people who are very rooted in our homes, but we often yearn for the freedom of the road outside.

My prayer

Dear Father, some mornings we feel in a better mood than others. The weather can be dreary, and this doesn't help us to feel our best. But on the dreary mornings help us together to have a sense of the joy of the Holy Trinity. We are people who love company and friendship and song, and we join ourselves with all these things that are at the heart of your life and our world. Send us good friends and help us to enjoy every minute of every day even when the weather is closing in. Amen

PART THREE

God is Kindly
and Close

Day 8

The God of Friendship

How wonderful is Thy friendliness toward me! How deep! How unchanging. Give me grace to pass it on.

Hebridean Altars[8]

Saviour and friend, how wonderful art Thou! My companion upon the changeful way. The comforter of its weariness. My guide to the eternal town. The welcome at its gate.

Hebridean Altars[9]

There have been many points in my life when other people's friendliness towards me has felt like a life-saver. In times when we feel wretched, being offered simple normal friendship is essential. Sometimes we just need to know that we are surrounded by friendly people who are happy for us to be ourselves. They reassure us that life is normal. In times like these, normality is a precious commodity.

Friendship is the great glue that sticks us together and patches us up. It is surely no accident that Jesus travelled with a group of friends on his great ministry. It was lonely enough going to the cross, but those months where he travelled as part of his ministry must have been made much better by the simple friendship of the other people he travelled with. Life is like that.

I can bring to mind many friends that I have had over the years. But it seems a bit more of a stretch to think of God as a friend. A distant heavenly father is a paradigm that is hard to shift, but the Celtic Christians had a beautiful sense of God as the gentle friend walking beside us, encouraging us and helping us when we feel low.

The first prayer poem talks about how deep and wonderful is God's friendship – or more particularly his friendliness. It's an interesting word because friendliness is something that feels easy and relaxed and the kind of thing that helps us to go about the world with a skip in our step.

The second prayer poem has, perhaps, a little more depth. It brings together Christ as the saviour and as the friend.

In J.R.R. Tolkien's *The Lord of the Rings* we encounter the reluctant hero, Aragorn. He has been part of the troop – its leader for most of the way. He goes on to become king – a far cry from the humble ranger of earlier in the saga. At his inauguration everyone kneels, but he goes to his friends, the hobbits and the others, and helps them to stand rather than kneel. He may be king, but they are also his friends.

The second prayer, with remarkable economy, gives us varying images of the friendliness of God. Christ is our companion. He is our companion on the changeful way. In these dark days we don't need anyone to tell us that life can be changeable – after all, the greatest change for decades is upon us. Christ is our comforter when we are weak – many of us can vouch for that. But it is the final image that I find the most interesting.

Christ, the poem prayer says, is our guide to the eternal town; the welcomer at its gate. It's very easy for the language of our faith to be prosaic and to be about propositional truth. I've heard too many talks that seem to be interested in ideas and theology but lack something of that ability to woo us towards the great story of the Christ. In just two short sentences, we get an image that is really intriguing. When one day we die and go to the eternal town, who will be there to welcome us at the gate? It will be our friend, Jesus. He will be there to welcome us home. And then he will be our guide to the eternal town.

He will show us round, he will make us feel at home; he will reassure us that this is just the next part of our journey. And we will know, we will know that God is for us and always has been.

Christ is always at the door waiting to be invited in. As the prayer has it:

I am a servant of God the Son at the door,
O! arise Thou thyself and open to me.

Carmina Gadelica, Prayer 68[10]

My prayer

Dear Father, banish any thoughts that you are a distant and angry God. Instead, help us to see your friendliness towards us and to revel in all that good friendship is. Our friends help us to get through the difficult times and share the good times with us and, Father, it is wonderful that you do just the same. Amen

---

Day 9

God is in the House

I lie down this night with God,
and God will lie down with me;
I lie down this night with Christ,
And Christ will lie down with me;
I lie down this night with the Spirit,
And the Spirit will lie down with me;
God and Christ and the Spirit
Be lying down with me.

Carmina Gadelica, Prayer 327[11]

It is perhaps a little daunting to think that the Trinity might move in with us someday. What would we have to do to accommodate them and would we always have to be on our best behaviour? Might it get a little crowded?

This little gem is an invocation of the Trinity and locates them as very close. It feels as though they are best friends and are very near to us.

It is charming to think that we might snuggle up with God and enjoy being thoroughly cared for and protected.

There is another Celtic prayer that's very similar to this. It also pictures a comforting domestic setting for God.

> *I lie down this night*
> *Near the king of life,*
> *Near Christ of the destitute,*
> *Near the Holy Spirit.*

Carmina Gadelica, Prayer 328[12]

I didn't know much about the faith for very many years. My family didn't go to church and although I was a bit interested in the Christian faith when I was quite young, by the time I was a teenager I'd lost all concern. Although I hadn't read the Bible or discussed Christianity with anyone, I had a lot of fixed ideas. I had created a straw man – a parody of God that no Christian would recognize. I didn't believe in that God; but then nor did they.

I had the idea that God was some kind of tyrant and uncaring with it. I certainly didn't think he was good company or that he might be close. I made the jump from the suffering in the world and reasoned that if God couldn't be bothered to get in and sort it then he wasn't worth thinking about at all. In some ways, it's easier to think of a God who is distant. That kind of God makes no demands upon us; that kind of God is no example. God is either asleep on the job or angry and unhappy with us.

The Celtic Christians had a charming and lovely sense that God is part of everyday life. He is in every detail of life and his good humour and kindliness are always on display. They certainly understood the power of God and that he is awesome, and they never took him for granted. However, they welcomed him into their homes and their everyday lives and saw him as their companion and friend. He was as likely to be in the kitchen as in the church – likely to be with the women as they milked the cows or took joy in contemplating their animals and livestock. Domestic life was infused with God.

This is the kind of God that inspires me. To put it bluntly, I can't see much point in a God who is unfriendly or distant. I could never be bullied into faith through fear of getting things wrong or of the punishments I might face. Like many modern people, I will be happy to take my chances and live the life that I want.

When we talk about the Celtic Christians having a sense of the homely and domestic God, we don't mean that he is domesticated. What we mean is that he is thrillingly close and that he enjoys our company. He is still the God of wonders and miracles. The Celtic Christians had a strong sense of God's might and desire for justice, but they held this together with a sense of his imminence and presence. Not just that he was hanging around watching us, like a spooky uncle; instead he is keenly interested in the events of our daily lives.

My prayer

Dear Father, what a beautiful thought that you have taken up residence with us in our homes. As we go about our daily business, you are there with us and enjoying all that we do as part of our labour. Help me to know that you are close and let this light up my day and night. There is so much to share and so much to celebrate and it is so good to know that you are there to do that with us. Amen

---

Day 10

God with Us as We Light the Fire

I will kindle my fire this morning
In presence of the holy angels of heaven,
In presence of Ariel of the loveliest form,
In presence of Uriel of the myriad charms,
Without malice, without jealousy, without envy,
Without fear, without terror of anyone under the sun,
But the Holy Son of God to shield me.

Carmina Gadelica, Prayer 82[13]

Sometimes, we think that we experience God mostly in church and then we forget about him during the rest of the week. It doesn't help that it's quite rare to hear a sermon in church about work and about the everyday lives of those who are turning up. It is all too easy to construct a holy part of our life that contains God and an earthly part that has everything else in it.

The Celtic Christians interwove their work and their labours with the presence of God. The kindling of the fire in the morning was a very important job. The fire had probably died down or been dampened down during the night and needed to be got going again, especially on those cold and difficult days. Here, the speaker kneels or stoops to get the kindling in place and to make sure the flame takes hold. At this very moment of normality, they know they're doing so in the presence of angels.

It is a rather lovely thought that as we go about our business, angels are watching us, standing with us and celebrating what we do. I can't be alone in wanting one day to meet with angels, to speak with them and to understand more about them. These creatures of glory and power are fascinating to me and to many others. In this prayer poem, the presence of these holy angels encourages the speaker to make commitments about the way they are going to live out the rest of their day.

They determine that they will live without malice, jealousy or envy, all of which will make for a happy community and a much happier day. It has been striking in these times of pestilence here that many of us have begun to wonder if we all need to be a great deal kinder to each other. In the days before it all started, there seemed to be a ratcheting up of invective and poison, especially on the Internet. We have seemed like a polarized and angry country. I can't be the only one to have been very uncomfortable with this and to despair about it at times. Where would it end, I began to wonder. It was certainly uncomfortable to witness the equivalent of people being dragged to the stocks and having rotten fruit thrown at them when they made an error of judgement in public.

When we go back to our Celtic forebears, we see that the simple act of lighting a fire and knowing that the holy angels are near helps the speaker to think about the way they live their life. They decide to live their life in a way that doesn't hurt others. They also take great comfort from God being so close; they know they can live without fear or terror because the Holy Son of God, Jesus, is there to shield them. The Celtic Christians lived in a way that acknowledged that we often experience something of the peace of God as we go about our daily lives. We sometimes put this down to just being over-sensitive, but perhaps we too can know that God is so close and that we experience him day by day.

I know that I become thin-skinned and difficult when I rely only upon my own resources. It is easy, especially when locked away like this, to begin to worry and to be fearful. But the Christian God of the Celts is in the very centre of our home, helping the hearth to be a place of warmth and welcome. Perhaps when we strike a match to light a candle, we might, too, experience his presence.

This kind of prayer poem is one of the reasons why so many feel that Celtic Christianity is like coming home. Most of us can be impressed by grand churches. We can enjoy the erudition of sermons. We can enjoy the rituals of church. None of these is wrong. But when Celtic spirituality takes us to a new dimension it helps us to feel that we are not alone and that God is not on our case but is here alongside us.

My prayer

Dear Father, be with me in all my daily tasks and duties. As I make the coffee in the morning and the breakfast, be close to me. As I do my household chores, be near. Help me to do my chores in a way that is honouring to you. I am joyous that you are close to me, and may I never take this closeness for granted. Amen

---

We Could Have a Glass of Ale
with Jesus

I would like to have the men of Heaven
in my own house;
with vats of good cheer
laid out for them.
I would like to have the three Marys,
their fame is so great.
I would like people
from every corner of Heaven.
I would like them to be cheerful
in their drinking.
I would like to have Jesus, too,
here amongst them.
I would like a great lake of beer
for the King of Kings.
I would like to be watching Heaven's family
Drinking it through all eternity.

Source unknown, ascribed to St Brigid

I think I would have liked St Brigid, the patron saint of beer and brewing. According to legend she was very fond of a pint of ale and was thought to have been the best brewer in the whole of Ireland. She is said to have supplied beer to eighteen churches out of one barrel, which then went on to last from Maundy Thursday to the end of Easter.

Brigid is also the patron saint of poets, students, blacksmiths, healers, cattle, dairymaids, midwives, fugitives, and children born out of wedlock. That is quite a portfolio and one I think any saint would be proud to have.

I, for one, love the image of quietly, beautifully, happily sitting and having a beer with Jesus. I do note that the beer appears to be in great quantities, but I imagine that having had a drink with our Lord resulted in no hangover in the morning!

Brigid is the classic Celtic saint, quirky and comforting. They must have been celebrating in heaven when she was born in 451.

I have sometimes wondered whether we need more feasting and merriment as part of the ongoing business of being part of a community and a church. Sometimes we could get together and just enjoy each other's company without needing to *do* anything. It is possible to get together without having a teaching session or strumming an acoustic guitar. Perhaps we might enjoy some ale and wine and exchange the stories of our lives.

This lovely prayer poem conjures the idea of merrymaking with the Christ. The closest I've ever come to this kind of thing was when I went to the old Soviet Republic of Georgia. I went along with my friend, Jonathan Aitken, to help run some sessions with Christian leaders from that country.

One evening, we were told that we were going out to a local village to enjoy the hospitality of the people there as a way of thanking us for our work. We got into cars and we left Tbilisi on the motorway. After a while the motorway gave way to small roads and then to a track, and the further we went, the more rural and poor things became. There were people riding on donkeys, and as we drove by they all stopped to wave at us. It struck me only later that the silent men in overcoats who accompanied us were our armed guards.

When we got to the village, we were ushered into the house of one of the elders. In the back room was a large table and many chairs with the view out into a large orchard and gardens. The table was piled with food and amazing delicacies. Every family in the village had contributed something and each of them wanted to show us something of their culture and their food. Being hospitable and of good cheer was an honour to them.

We hear in the Bible of there being a banquet in heaven. This was the closest I have come to it on earth. The food was simply magnificent. And between each course we stopped to drink a small shot of vodka and make a toast. At one point, I asked if I might have a glass of beer. The host looked disapproving, and I wondered if I had upset him. A few minutes later he came back into the room with a huge smile on his face, carrying three separate glasses each containing one litre of local beer.

It was truly a glorious event. The food and the alcohol spoke of good times. During the evening, I spoke to one of the elders who told me what life had been like under the Communists. He told me that they had tried to crush the faith in the villages of Georgia. Their own priest was taken away and killed. The state thought that they had eliminated Christianity, but they had not taken account of one thing.

Despite the surveillance and the punishments, the villagers met in each other's houses and shared food and drink, hospitality and love. It was in these extended family gatherings that they were able to keep the faith alive and worship the Lord through the ministry of good cheer, story-telling and being together.

At one point in the evening, I enquired about whether I might use the facilities. With a glint in his eye, the villager told me that I'd have to go down to the outside toilet in the garden, and to be careful because only yesterday a wolf had been sleeping by the door.

My prayer

Dear Father, you are the God of good times and good cheer. Jesus turned water into wine; and great wine at that. You like it when we have merry times and company and song. You take pleasure in our gentle pleasures. Thank you for the taste and comforts of ale and that you join us in our friendships. We raise a glass to you and celebrate good cheer and good will to all. Amen

---

PART FOUR

Our Animal Friends

Day 12

God is in the Creation

There is no bird on the wing;
There is no star in the skies;
There is nothing beneath the sun
But forth Thy goodness cries;
Jesus, Jesus, Jesus
Thou art our soul's high prize.

Hebridean Altars[14]

Long before I became a Christian, I think I was having intimations of God. Later on I would describe it by saying that God was on my case. This didn't come from going to church or reading a Bible. Instead, I regularly had a sense of awe and wonderment when being in the natural world.

I have always had a great affinity for garden birds.When I was growing up in Northolt, there always seemed to be plenty of sparrows, blackbirds and starlings. It has been a great sadness that the lovely little sparrows seem to be in sharp decline.

I remember that my mum and dad would always leave out food for the birds and we'd sometimes sit at our back window, all of us watching our feathered friends and marvelling at them. Northolt is quite a built-up place. It certainly isn't the Cotswolds. Our neighbours tended to work at the airport. It is one of those forgotten suburbs. But you can't keep the creation out from anywhere. Even in Northolt, with the A40 thundering through, the birds were always around.

Seeing God in nature is called 'natural theology' and it is one of the gateways to the faith. Many people might wrestle with the way we do church and some of our teachings, but let them spend some time in their garden and feel the strange peace that this brings; it opens them up to wonderment, and perhaps the source of that wonder.

This little Celtic jewel makes a bold claim. Every bird, every star, everything in the created universe says something of the goodness of Jesus.

> There is nothing beneath the sun
> But forth Thy goodness cries;
> Jesus, Jesus, Jesus.

I like the idea that nature reveals God's goodness. Of course, we know that nature can be cruel though. We live in an imperfect world. But our Celtic forebears lived close to nature and wouldn't dream of exploiting it in the way that we have. Of course, there was no factory farming or mass production, and animals both wild and domestic were cherished. They were cherished not just for practical reasons; the family would rely on its cows and goats for milk. Creatures were cherished because they were precious to the Creator and had to be respected, it was our duty. If we disrespected animals then we disrespected the Creator who sustains them and us through the power of the Holy Spirit.

Some time ago I went to Lindisfarne, Holy Island. I remember walking across the causeway and feeling a great sense of peace. The highlight of my trip was sitting in a café in the small village on the island and watching birds hop and flutter in and out of a tree in the garden. It transported me, and nature has delighted many over the years.

Yesterday, I noticed a flash of colour in the oak tree just outside my window. One of the highlights of living here has been watching that tree over time. It is like a city with its own rules and activity. Squirrels nest there, as do birds. An owl sometimes lands on one of the large branches and stays for a while. Pigeons stay a few minutes and the insects are always present. Yesterday, we were visited by a beautiful jay. I marvelled at its plumage and how unconcerned it seemed. This lovely little bird seemed like a gift and a reminder that the world is still a beautiful place.

I have a story about the way the natural world can reveal something of God's love to us and make us feel better. In some ways, I'm a little ashamed because this story does point to a slight flimsiness of faith on my part. On Good Friday, we regularly take part in a walk of witness. A few hundred Christians walk up into the town near us each year. I must confess that I find it a rather dismal affair. I often wonder what I would have made of it if I was not a Christian and I was in one of those cars held up in the queue behind us. It perhaps might be better if we looked cheerful, but on this day we're encouraged to say nothing and walk in silence.

I was a non-Christian for a very long time and sometimes I feel back in touch with the way I was then. One thing I know is that a walk of witness would never have encouraged me to go into church and might have confirmed my prejudice that Christians were humourless killjoys. Friends of mine in the clergy tell me that the purpose of the walk is as an act of worship and one of the few we do in public each year. Of course, I accept that. But in this particular year, I was feeling so gloomy with the way that it was going that about three-quarters of the way around I decided to come home.

The sun was shining and so I sat in my garden with a cup of tea. I was soon joined by a robin that was sitting no more than two feet away from me. He was looking at me and I was looking at him. Perhaps he was as fascinated with me as I was with him. He was very beautiful. The robin is the garden bird that is least afraid of us humans and so we get very close to them and we feel very close to them.

As the robin and I looked at each other I began to feel a great sense of peace and calm. This little bird was ministering to me because it made me realize just how wonderful the world is and how grateful I am to God. This year the walk of witness was cancelled, which may help me develop some stamina for it next year. We shall see.

My prayer

Dear Father, thank you for the creatures that we share our world with. Thank you that when we see them, we know that the world is good and that you made it. Help us to be good stewards of this precious world and to appreciate all that is around us. In times of difficulty help us to take comfort from the creatures we share our world with and to see them as brothers and sisters rather than as things to be exploited or ignored. Amen

Day 13

God and the Creatures

Thanks to Thee ever, O gentle Christ,
That Thou hast raised me freely from the black
And from the darkness of last night
To the kindly light of this day.
Praise unto Thee, O God of all the creatures,
According to each life Thou hast poured on me,
My desire, my word, my sense,
My thought, my deed, my way.

Carmina Gadelica, Prayer 224[15]

Good morning, dear friends. I am sitting in my vicarage and the sun is streaming in through the windows. The tulips are springing to life and yesterday the red kite was back circling on the thermals. Each day I go into the garden to say hello to my little robin friend. And my cats sleep comfortably for most of the day. The rhythms of life are a great comfort in difficult times.

Our relationship with animals can be complicated. I struggle with the idea of eating meat, but I still do it. But animals have given me great consolation over the years and especially in times when things seem uncertain. I enjoy their company and I find myself thrilled at their beauty.

I share my house with three cats. In the normal run of things, I'm often on my own in the house apart from my cat friends and so I get a great deal of time to look at them and them to look at me. Many people tell me that in tough times their pets have been a source of reassurance to them. It encourages me to think of God as the God of all creatures.

This little prayer begins from a place of darkness and moves into the light. The bedrock of the prayer is the acknowledgement of the gentleness of Jesus and that we have life each day only as a result of his being. This leads to gratitude. The day is full of kindly light. I need to remind myself of this sometimes.

The Celtic story is full of wonderful tales of the Celtic saints developing strong and lasting ties with animals and forming deep friendships with them. It is interesting that in Mark's Gospel, Jesus too formed great bonds with animals during his time in the wilderness. Ian Bradley in *The Celtic Way* reports that St Serf had a pet robin and a lamb that followed him around and raised a dead pig to life. Ciaran was helped in the graveyard by a tame wild boar that helped him to dig the graves. In time he employed the boar as his servant. St Cuthbert, as mentioned earlier, had his life saved by wild animals on a number of occasions and the sea otters would dry and warm his legs when he had been praying all night in the water.

I have a strong sense that animals honour God just by being themselves. When we see an animal in all its glory living life as it should be, we don't just see the glory of God in them; by being themselves they are celebrating God in their own way.

I am most fond of the eighteenth-century poet, journalist and Anglican, Christopher Smart. His poem, 'Jubilate Agno', explains the way his precious cat Jeoffry is part of creation's celebration of God.

For I will consider my Cat Jeoffry.
For he is the servant of the Living God duly and daily serving him.
For at the first glance of the glory of God in the East he worships in his Way.
For this is done by wreathing his body seven times round with elegant quickness.
For then he leaps up to catch the musk, which is the blessing of God upon his prayer.[15]

Unfortunately, Smart ended up in a lunatic asylum, but that was nothing to do with his views on cats and creation. His great insight was that animals, in their way, worship the Creator. When we take pleasure in their antics, we also see God at work, if only we look closely enough. I can't resist another short excerpt from Smart's poem. I, for one, find it hard to disagree with him. Most cat owners would probably agree as well.

For he purrs in thankfulness, when God tells him he is a good cat.
For he is an instrument for children to learn benevolence upon.
For every house is incomplete without him and a blessing is lacking in the spirit.

My prayer

Dear Father, thank you for the creatures that we share our homes with. Thank you for our pets. We get so much enjoyment and love from them and, when we watch them, we see much of your goodness acted out in their lives. Help us to be kind to animals and to see them as a great gift from you, especially when we are sad or in difficult times. Amen

Day 14

The Theology of Admiring Creation

Look at the animals roaming the forest; God's spirit dwells within them. Look at the birds flying across the sky: God's spirit dwells within them. Look at the tiny insects crawling in the grass: God's spirit dwells within them. Look at the fish in the river and the sea, God's spirit dwells within them. There is no creature on earth in whom God is absent.

Pelagius, 'Letter to an Elderly Friend'[17]

Pelagius was the great theologian of the Celtic world. He was a large and ungainly man and had a knack of making enemies – none more so than St Augustine. He was condemned as a heretic although this is rather harsh. Careful reading of his work reveals nothing of the kind. But he was an optimist in an age of pessimists, and this didn't help him. He believed in original goodness.

Pelagius' letter is more like a poem than prose. It is as lyrical as the creation that he describes. He asks us to take on board the evidence of our own eyes. We are encouraged to use our senses and our brains in order to get closer to God. Pelagius says that the evidence is clear and all around us, we just need to look out for it and be sensitive to it. I have no difficulty in believing that our planet is both special and made by God.

Pelagius looks at the animals in the forest and *knows* that God's Spirit is in them. He realizes the same is true of the birds and the insects and the fish. The Holy Spirit, the giver of life, is in all things. This helps us to see the world afresh and maybe encourages us to think again about the way we treat our planet and the animals, insects and flora that we share it with.

During lockdown, we are having our vegetables delivered. I say this shamefacedly, but we used to waste a great deal of food. It would get put in the fridge and then we would discover that it was out of date or gone off. We are now taking our food much more seriously and making sure we don't waste any. I so hope that this continues over the coming years. As well as our food, I'm finding myself more and more grateful for the natural world around me.

If we imagine that the character of the Holy Spirit is joy, creativity, peacefulness, happiness and the like, then we begin to see that the animals and creatures we share our world with are especially precious. If they too are filled with this Holy Spirit, then we do well to honour them and treat them well. St Francis used to call the creatures his brothers and sisters and he meant it. I wonder how life would be different if we took the same point of view.

You might find this fanciful, but I have no doubt that during times of trouble, stress and pain in my family our cats seem to have an instinct that they need to comfort us. When we are ill, they seem to spend most of the day at our side. They lie at the entrance to our bedroom to guard us when we seem stressed and they seem to know exactly the right time to come and be near us. You might think that this is the worst kind of anthropomorphism. I do understand.

But if it is true that the animals and everything that we share our world with is full of life-giving Holy Spirit, then it wouldn't be such a stretch of the imagination to see our animal friends as our companions and our protectors.

This ancient Scottish prayer, whose author is unknown, is a beauty.

And may the blessing of the Earth be on you
The great round earth; may you ever have
A kindly greeting for them you pass
As you're going along the roads.
May the earth be soft under you when you rest upon it,
Tired at the end of the day,
And may it rest easy over you when,
At the last, you lay out under it;
May it rest so lightly over you,
That your soul may be out from under it quickly,
And up, and off, and on its way to God

My prayer

Dear Father, help us to see the deep truth of our ancient forebears. They understood how the created world revealed the beauty of the Creator. Help us to share this insight with others and to take pleasure in the wonderful world that we live in, even when things are difficult and hard. Amen

Day 15

Everything Connects

So Excellence of corn,
Excellence of drink,
Excellence of music,
Excellence of guiding,
Excellence of sea and land be thine.
Excellence of sitting,
Excellence of journeying,
Excellence of cattle,
Excellence of churning,
Excellence of curds and butter be thine.

Carmina Gadelica, Prayer 278[18]

This comes from a section called the 'Invocation of the Graces'. To 'invoke' is to ask for something, to make a plea for it. It also has the hint of bringing something into being, of making it happen.
I tend to only plead for things when I am making an emergency prayer when everything has gone wrong. But this prayer plea above is

pleasing because it comes from a happy place – it was perhaps issued on behalf of a couple about to marry. If that was the case, a lot of this can translate directly to today. Who wouldn't wish good food, drink, music and guidance upon a new couple? I wish someone had invoked such things for my wife and me when we married. It certainly shows a sense of relaxed benevolence.

It may not be only about creation, but it does have an important mention of animals and their part in our lives. Let us look at the sequence. The speaker begins by acknowledging the excellence of having a relaxed sociable time. In times of peril it is just this kind of thing that we miss the most. In my experience, it isn't the big things that I have been missing in the last few weeks. What I miss most is being in the company of my friends and family and the ability to get out and see some of the beautiful places around near where I live.

The speaker acknowledges the importance of rest and the need for blessing in times of journeys. It would be so easy to end the prayer poem here but there's more and it shows the real breadth of vision of the Celtic Christians.

Having set what might be called a domestic agenda, the invocation moves on to cover some of the things that are so important to life. The speaker invokes the importance of cattle and of churning the milk, of making butter and the things that are needed for food and survival. This little prayer puts our animal friends in the wider context of our entire lives.

We are citizens of the world and we share that world with other people, other species and all of creation. The Celtic Christians help us to count our blessings and ask for more. It is refreshing that they don't compartmentalize nature and keep it away from the rest of life. The cow, the sea, the sky and the birds are all intrinsically linked. We're in this together and the sooner we see it and live like it the better.
Not many of us these days have cattle and very few of us churn the milk, although we might have to if the nation runs out of food. If we

were writing this today, we would still want to invoke all the good things in our lives. That might include pets as well as the wild animals around us. It isn't that long ago that, here in Brent, the farmer would move his cattle each day across the road and into Northwick Park.

My prayer

Dear Father, thank you for our food and thank you for the farmers who grow it. Thank you for people who pick the crops and package them and for our retailers. Please never let us take for granted the food that we have; let's prepare it carefully and not waste it. Amen

---

PART FIVE

Healing

Day 16

When Illnesses are Driving Us Half-mad

The incantation put by lovely Bride
before the thumb of the Mother of God,
On lint, on wort, on hemp,
For worm, for venom, for teeth.
The worm that tortured me,
In the teeth of my head,
hell hard by my teeth,
The teeth of hell distressing me.
The teeth of hell close to me;
As long as I myself shall last
May my teeth last in my head.

Carmina Gadelica, Prayer 126[19]

If you have ever suffered from a raging toothache, you know that it is a pain that is very hard to put up with. No pain is good pain, but tooth pain is particularly devilish. Or as this prayer poem has it – the pain is hellish. We say, Amen to that.

Where this prayer has got it right is that it does not duck away from the real nature of the distress. Sometimes we can be just too polite. I always think that when we pray to God for healing and in our distress, we should let it all hang out. What is the point of trying to pretend things are OK or minimizing our problems when we just want to say that we are in pain and in trouble?

I'm not sure if the writer of this prayer was aiming to raise a smile, but they have certainly done it. It amuses me not just that they are praying for the end of pain, but they would like, for as long as they live, to have teeth in their heads. Take the pain, but for God's sake leave me the teeth. They may have been rural people in a time not obsessed by fashion, but it seems that the desire not to be gummy, runs right throughout the ages.

Losing teeth is no fun. Once, the crown on my front tooth fell out on the way to the airport as we headed off on holiday. To begin with it was funny. But after a few days of not being able to eat or speak properly, the novelty wore off. Teeth are like that.

There is certainly something charming in the way the prayer is put, and I shall forever call a toothache, 'the teeth of hell'.

My prayer

Our dear Father, help us to be honest when we are suffering. Help us to tell you and others when we are in distress and pain. Help us to know that we aren't superhuman and that sometimes we get sick and need help. Amen

Day 17

The Shinbone's Connected to the . . .

Deliver my skull, hair-covered head, and eyes,
Mouth, tongue, teeth and nostrils,
Neck, breast, side and limbs,
Joints, fat and two hands.
To my chin, beard, eyebrows, ears,
Chaps, cheeks, septum, nostrils,
Pupils, irises, eyelids, and the like,
To gums, breath, jaws, gullet . . .
Protect my spine and ribs and their joints,
Back, ridge, and sinews with their bones;
Protect my skin and blood with kidneys,
The area of the buttocks, nates with thighs.
Protect my hams, calves, femurs,
Houghs and knees with knee-joints;
Protect my ankles and shins and heels,
Shanks, feet with their soles.

Protect my toes growing together,
With the tips of the toes and twice five nails;
Protect my breast, collarbone and small breast,
Nipples, stomach, and navel.

Seventh-century Irish, 'The Breastplate of Laidcenn'

I think that this prayer poem is difficult to beat. I am a bit vague sometimes when I pray for healing for myself or others. Although I do remember a parishioner who collared me at the door of the church on the way out from a service. He asked me to pray for his haemorrhoids, which I felt was a bit too much detail. I didn't quite know what to pray or indeed whether to look him in the eye. I suppose it was a compliment that he felt relaxed enough with me to mention his condition.

When I pray, I tend to mention a general condition or perhaps some general things that would be *nice* for God to attend to, if he could possibly find the time. Our Celtic forebears were able to create a spectacular list of body parts in their prayers and they are all the better for it.

I must confess that I have no idea what Chaps are, or Houghs. It might be indelicate to speculate. There aren't many modern prayers for the buttocks, nates or thighs but perhaps there should be more. I certainly have never come across a prayer that lists so many different parts of the body. In some way it is a wonder of human biology – a map of our component parts (and I have edited the prayer down for length . . . the original is much longer).

I think we might all join in with the prayer for the protection of our toes and the hope that they may not grow together. I may even join in with a prayer for the navel although it isn't an area I have considered much since the day of my birth.

To be serious for a moment though – this prayer understands that prevention is as good as cure. It calls down the breastplate of protection on our bodies and that can never be a bad thing.

We live in an age of extraordinary advances in medicine and surgery. Our forebears would have needed to rely on relatively primitive ways of healing, although they had a much better idea of how to use herbs and other tinctures. We tend to compartmentalize medicine and as such we get treated for individual parts of our body by individual specialists. This prayer, though, throws in the baby as well as the bath water, and names – in glorious fashion – the bits that make up the body. It is a beautiful litany of the human form.

I detect it is not just a fascination with body parts but a deep admiration for the way the body is put together. We are awesome creatures made up of chemicals, bones, electricity and pumps. We are also more than the sum of our parts because we have consciousness; the ghost in the machine. It is intriguing that this prayer has such a long list of elements that it is praying for protection and restoration of. My feeling is that our Celtic brothers and sisters were fascinated by the construction of the human body because they were clear who was the great builder. In recent times we have become much more focused on our own National Health Service. We have been reminded again about the skill of our doctors, nurses, healthcare workers and other professionals. We realize that our life may depend upon the work that they do, and that is something which many of us have not had to think of before.

In this time of contagion and fear we are keenly aware about the dangers of infection. The Celtic people experienced plague and I now know the fear that it brought. They could be well in the morning and have died by the time of their evening meal. This kind of thing tends to make our prayers for healing more specific and more urgent.

My prayer

Father, thank you for those who look after us. We are sorry if we have undervalued them in the past, and we will make up for this in the future. Help us to cherish our bodies in all their different parts and to know that we need protecting. Help us to see the Maker in the made and to revel at the complexity and beauty of our bodies. Amen

---

Day 18

Jesus the Physician

O most gentle Physician, Thou hast a balsam for each hurt of ours, be it from ourselves or from another. Thou feelest our spirit's pain in Thine. For Thou and we are kin so close that none can be closer. Therefore it is Thy delight to heal us.

Hebridean Altars[20]

During the emergency that we're living through, we're all getting a new reminder of how amazing our National Health Service is. Nurses and doctors are putting themselves at risk to help us. It is hard not to be moved by the example of many tens of thousands of people who are working to save other people, putting their own lives at risk to treat people they don't even know.

It was telling that when the Prime Minister, Boris Johnson, returned home, after narrowly escaping with his life, he reflected on the NHS and the care that he received. He said that at the heart of the NHS is an indivisible heartbeat. That heartbeat is love. I've never heard a politician speak in such a way and it was good to hear. Carers, nurses, doctors and all those who work to restore health in other people are among the real heroes of our age.

Over the years, I have been blessed by having some tremendous doctors to look after me. The best of them combine being calm and knowledgeable but also have genuine compassion. Head and heart work together.

When a very close family member was desperately ill in hospital having suffered a brain haemorrhage, it was a horrific time for us. One Saturday morning I was in hospital visiting her, and we were both scared. During my visit, the neurosurgeon who had been treating her came in. It was his day off, but he wanted to come and see how she was. That meant a great deal to us and it still does.

We all pray for healing; it comes with the territory of being a Christian. I believe very strongly that the Lord heals and have seen examples in my life and the life of those around us.

I respond very positively to the idea of Christ as the great physician. After all, everyone needs healing. Sometimes what ails us is obvious to all; but sometimes our brokenness is hidden and not so obvious. Had Christ just come to preach a message or lay out a manifesto, it is hard to believe that his ministry would have got beyond those first few years.

Christ was a teacher *and* a healer. Why did the great physician heal people? I believe he did so not so much to prove a point, but more because he was moved and could not walk by on the other side of the road. He healed because he could do nothing other than that. As the Celtic prayer asserts – it is Christ's delight to heal us. He does it for us because he can.

All of us sometimes feel distant from God. Prayer can sometimes be difficult, and we wonder how to sustain our faith. When I am feeling bad or ill, I remind myself that Jesus is the greatest doctor that ever was. He can set the prisoners free, and that means the prisoners of illness, both physical and mental.

I would be intrigued to know what medical care was available to people when this prayer was written. What is certain is that they had a high regard for physicians. In an age without antibiotics or mass-produced pain-killers, how did they cope? What medicines did the doctors bring? So often, it is the doctor who is the cure.

In this lovely prayer poem, the image is of Christ, the great physician, but also as one of our kin. Christ is so close to us; he is as close as the closest person we have in our family. It is as though a family member is also a doctor and so will pay special attention to us.

My prayer

*Jesus, please draw near to us when we are
lonely or ill. Reassure us that we are part of your
beautiful family and that you will never let us go.
We entrust ourselves into your care and know that
closeness with you can only be for the good. Amen*

Day 19

We Pray Only When We are in Distress

In the day of thy health,
Thou wilt not give devotion,
Thou wilt not give kine,
Nor wilt thou offer incense . . .
But thy winter will come,
And the hardness of thy distress,
And thy head shall be as
the clod in the earth.
Thy strength having failed,
Thy aspect having gone
And thou a thrall,
On thy two knees.

Carmina Gadelica, Prayer 207[21]

The Celtic Christians did not have their heads in the clouds. They were realistic about each other and the way we frequently let God down.

They just weren't obsessed with it. But they weren't soft on the consequences of sin; who could be? This little prayer expresses the way they balance hope and realism.

> *Take me often from the tumult of things into Thy presence. There show me what I am and what Thou hast purposed me to be. Then hide me from Thy tears.*
>
> *Hebridean Altars*[22]

This little prayer is another one that has the feel of a proverb about it. It has a level of distilled wisdom that is useful to us and describes some of the barriers we all face. Here is one of the most common of them. When life is going well, we seem to forget to pray. It is a common issue and all of us, I am sure, have fallen foul of this.

But we need to read the prayer very carefully and not find condemnation when it isn't there. If we read it carefully, the fault is not simply forgetting to pray when things are going well; it's a stubborn resistance to giving any credit to God for all that he is and does.

It is the stubbornness of refusing to say thank you in the good times that is the most hurtful to God. Jesus has the same thing in his own ministry. At one point a group of lepers comes up and he heals them all and yet only one comes back to say thank you. At the very least, forgetting to say thank you is a breach of manners.

The prayer has a rather ominous ending, or at least a dose of realism. It forecasts that those people who sail through life without feeling any need to be in touch with God will one day be brought to their knees with their strength gone.

In these terrible times I wonder how many prayers have been spoken. There's absolutely nothing wrong with praying in distress. Indeed, what else would we do in such circumstances? I was touched to hear that the government's cabinet all prayed for Boris Johnson when he was at risk of losing his life. Praying when everything looks lost is the most natural thing in the world. After all, when Christ feels desolate, he cries out a prayer to God, wondering why his father has deserted him. This prayer of desolation is one we perhaps all have had cause to utter at some point in our life.

My guess is you'd find very few atheists if you were on an aircraft that began to have engine failure. I think we'd all be praying in those circumstances. God hears our prayers and understands our difficulties with them. Some people are simply better at it than others. Some have a gift for it. But for those of us who find that praying doesn't always come naturally, then I'm sure that God understands that we do our best, and he honours that.

But this little prayer offers a useful nudge in the right direction. When we are well, and our health is good, why not give thanks for it? When we wake and some pains are gone and we feel full of life, why not be joyous? And when we can be active and do all the things we want, why not see this as a gift rather than a right?

All of us have our days when we are healthy, and for all of us one day our strength will fail. I pray that when I meet my Maker, he will know that I thanked him in my good times, as well as my bad. That I gave him due credit, not because I felt forced to, but because I wanted to.

My prayer

Father, for when my resolve fails or when I forget to come to you, forgive me. In my busyness and lack of attention to you, forgive me. When I am well, let me know that you are the source of my wellness. If I forget you, please do not forget me.
Amen

PART SIX

We are Open to a
Powerful Joy

Day 20

Clinging to an Everyday Joy

As the hand is made for holding and the eye for seeing, Thou hast fashioned me for joy. Share with me the vision that shall find it everywhere: in the wild violet's beauty; in the lark's melody; in the face of the steadfast man; in a child's smile; in a mother's love; in the purity of Jesus.

Hebridean Altars[23]

As I have grown older, my priorities have changed. As in any life, there have been ups and downs. I am not one who thinks that whatever doesn't kill us makes us stronger. No way. Sometimes bad stuff remains bad stuff and a stumbling block. Sometimes I have struggled to be cheerful and to be hopeful. That is part of my story. I've often wondered what the secret of a joyful life is. Sometimes you meet people who have had the most terrible tragedy and yet they managed to hang on to a central sense of joy and that life was worth living.

This little prayer is also a piece of ancient wisdom. It would fit well within the context of the Old Testament proverbs, those ancient bits of Jewish folk wisdom. The prayer is grounded in much thought about the nature and roots of joy. And as we ponder this, we need to be aware that the circumstances of people's lives, in the days after the Roman Empire crumbled, were very difficult. Joy was no easier then than it is now.

Just to grow enough food to feed one's family would have been a struggle and in years when the crops failed, hunger would be widespread. Illness had the capacity to wipe out whole communities. It was a time of tremendous political instability and that meant that the regular people were really on a knife edge, not knowing whether the king they had would be able to protect them. In these circumstances, joy must run alongside contingency. But perhaps that is its great secret. Joy does not come with a settled life with no problems; instead it is the currency of a life well-lived, problems and all.

In less than seventy words, we get a master-class in joy. Let us make our way through it carefully. In the same way that the hand is designed to hold something, and the eyes are to see something, we have been made or, as the speaker says, fashioned for joy. This is a bold statement and an optimistic one. It is very easy to be worn down by the fluctuations of life. Sometimes church has a habit of emphasizing all that is wrong with us rather than all that is right. But here we see that the very centre of life is an innate inalienable impetus towards joy. If we were to stop here that would give us enough food for thought, but there is more.

God has fashioned us with the seed of joy. How do we experience it and where do we find it? Within this prayer poem we find it in the everyday business, a miracle of life, we find it in nature, in the wild violet's beauty and in the singing of the lark. We find it in our relations with honourable men and women. Those who refuse to give up on us and continue to fight the good fight in the face of whatever opposition there is. We see it in the smile of a child and in the love of a mother, and of course, we see it too in the beautiful life of Jesus.

It would be easy to say these are too simplistic. But the older I get, the more I realize that it's in the simple things that we begin to see the essence of the big thing.

The Celts may have lived simple lives, but they were not simplistic people. They understood deep truths about the faith and how to find contentment. These ancient thoughts make very interesting reading in our current circumstances of the lockdown. Of course, by the time you read this we may be back out in the world, but at this moment we have the chance to wonder what it is that makes for our happiness.

Many things have surprised me about this time. Some of the things I thought I'd miss, I haven't missed at all. I don't really miss sport; I don't miss going shopping. I think that perhaps I was simply distracting myself from being bored. I do miss going to church, and I do miss having time with my family and friends. I've come to realize that there are certain groups of things that are essential for a happy life, a joyous life, and our Celtic forebears were on the money when it came to identifying them.

Who knows what will happen to our society when we begin to get back to normal? Will we go on as we did before? I do hope not. I hope that we begin to see that serving others and sacrificial love are at the heart of the whole business of being a human being. I hope we might tackle some of the inequalities in our society. I hope we might spend more time appreciating what we have rather than what we don't have. I hope that we still enjoy a moment's peace listening to the birds and being in awe of the beautiful planet that we live on.

My prayer

Father, we sometimes struggle to find joy in our everyday lives. Problems crowd in on us and the future looks uncertain. We wonder where our hope comes from, especially when we lose those who we love or when we feel we have let ourselves down. Unlock in us a powerful everyday joy and contentment and marry it with gratitude to you. Amen

---

Day 21

What Makes for the Joyous Life?

I pray for thee a joyous life,
Honour, estate and good repute,
No sigh from thy breast,
No tear from thine eye.
No hindrance on thy path,
No shadow on thy face,
Until thou lie down in that mansion,
In the arms of Christ benign.

Carmina Gadelica, Prayer 283[24]

I wonder how often we pray for joyous life for those around us. I spend a good deal of time praying for them to be healed and time saying prayers of gratitude. However, I don't spend much time praying for the joyous life of others.

It's a bit of a mystery really. I wonder if the reason that I don't pray these prayers is that I'm a little shy about it. The idea of joy is not the first one that comes to mind each morning when I pray and, in this, I can learn a great deal from the Celtic Christians.

What I like about this prayer is it identifies living a good life and having a good reputation among those we live with, which is an important part of joy. The work we do for others and the way in which we do it builds our reputation, and a good reputation is something to be cherished.

I grew up working in my parents' family business. We ran a hardware shop in the town in which we lived and like all shop owners we became very much part of the community we served. Everyone who came to the shop got a warm welcome and, because it was a family business, we prided ourselves on our honesty and good customer service. What we had was our good name in this community. Had we lost that, it would have been exceptionally painful for all of us. This prayer recognizes that having a good name is something that is hard won and something to be truly grateful for. The prayer is lavish in what it asks for, and indeed the request is, if anything, a little improbable. None of us will have the kind of life that this describes. We will always have problems and sometimes things will go wrong. But what is behind this prayer is an interesting impulse; the impulse to wish the very best for others.

The prayer encompasses the great sweep of life right through to our death. The image of lying down with Jesus with his arm around us is a very powerful one. But more powerful is it doesn't position joy only as something to come at the end of life. Joy is an accompaniment to life and something that God wants for us.

My prayer

Father, we want to be known as honourable and true because you are both of these in your very nature. Help us to rise above pettiness and focus our lives on serving others. Help us to see that joy comes in service and not other kinds of achievement. Help us to detect shards of joy in every situation. Amen

---

Day 22

The Joy That is Around Us

I set up on the shore, Father, watching the face of the waters and the sun-bright clouds; and the mystery of being stills my heart to awe. Then I think of Thee, and then, though mystery lingers, my fear of it is gone. I say to myself that beyond the empires of space and light, reaches Thy power to be my friend. Wherever I go, whether through a strange land or upon the dark sea-breast, Thou art with me. Therefore, I may be quiet of mind.

Hebridean Altars[25]

I think this might be the very best prayer reflection I have ever read on the nature of joy. We can make this kind of thing very complicated but reading this we begin to see the basis of joy and that we do not need to run away from its mysteries.

As is often the way, the rumination begins from a *real* place and a *real* time – before exploring a set of ideas. The speaker is sitting on the shore looking out at the waters. It is something we have all done. As he does this, he begins to think of God, the Father, and he begins to feel a little uncertain. What is he to make of what he is seeing in front of him? Maybe he suddenly feels very small in the face of the great scope of nature; the word we have for this is 'awestruck'. Nature is magnificent and timeless, but we are trapped in time and our lives are short. The seas will be raging and the rivers flowing long after we are no more.

When we are confronted by the majesty of nature, we wonder what our own life adds up to. Thankfully, the speaker realizes that the only way to quench his existential fear is to fall back on God. He says to himself that beyond all this extraordinary expanse is the power of God, who is his friend. That is a reassuring thought for all of us.

It is quite wonderful the way this short paragraph pivots at this point. It is a moment of clarity and epiphany. He realizes that wherever he goes, strange land or not, God is with him, and this leads to a profound sense of peace.

Joy can take many forms. It can be ecstatic. But it can also be this deep sense of oneness with God and with the world that we live in. In our busy lives it is very difficult to get to this kind of space. At times of stress and worry, we tend to be focused inwards rather than outwards and we can become frightened.

I remember on many occasions sitting on the sea wall at Minehead, looking out at the Bristol Channel with my father. He always told me that he felt a great sense of peace when I was there with him, and when we were looking out on this great scene. I only understand this love now that I am a parent too – I feel the same way about my daughters. Their company brings me a sense of peace as well.

Very shortly before my father died, he became a Christian, and we sat and talked to each other and read the Bible. We were able to talk about the times in our life when we felt this sense of peace and joy. I cherished those times and, in this prayer, I see deep truth about the nature of human happiness.

My prayer

*Father, so often a sense of peace is hard to find.
We rush, we worry, and we don't take time to see
what is right in front of us. In this very day, help us
to appreciate your world and all that is in it. Let us
take comfort in those that we love. Let us be like
still waters, at peace with who we are and who
you are. Amen*

Day 23

Beginning, Middle, End

As it was,
As it was,
As it shall be
Evermore,
O Thou triune
Of grace!
With the ebb,
With the flow . . .

Carmina Gadelica, Poem 216[26]

One of the objections that has been raised about the Celtic Christians is that they have more than a whiff of the New Age about them. One friend of mine said he found them too rural and their works didn't really apply to city life. Others have worried that the doctrine in their verse and prayers might be too unorthodox. I don't really think that either of these two things are true.

The Celtic Christians were people of their own time, dealing with the issues that were theirs. But there is never a ducking of the ruinous nature of sin, and the Celtic Christians had a way of never splitting the Trinity. The Trinity are together always when it comes to Celtic prayers and this is a very healthy corrective when we become too focused on either Father, Spirit or Son.

The Celts were a highly practical people. They had to be. They had no NHS to rely on, very few government structures and when things went wrong, they had to fix them themselves. Many of their amazing prayers and poems are about everyday life, the tiny details of farming or being with family and friends. That is why they're so appealing to many of us modern folk who long to see how our faith is applied to our life. We get a sense of a faith that was lived and that helped our forebears to live life to the full. We want to reclaim God in the everyday; I am sure of it.

There is, however, a mystical edge to some of the Celtic Christians' work. There is a sense that everything connects and that we do well to see the great interconnectedness of all things. This fragment of a prayer is perhaps one of the more mystical on offer.

Many people are familiar with the Celtic knot as a symbol. It is interesting because everything links; there is a sense of flow, an organic connectivity between everything, and that very much reflects the life that the Celtic Christians lived. It taps into some of our deepest yearnings in today's world where we sometimes feel alienated from each other and from our planet. I, at least, feel that we are an atomized society.

This fragment neatly pulls together this sense of connectedness. It implies, at least, that joy is not a commodity, but it is in fact deep within the DNA of the world. There are ebbs and flows in every life and yet in the end all things will work for the good.

Everything that ever was, is, and shall be is under the encompassing of the Holy Trinity. This is deeply comforting because it means that we are part of the great story of redemption. All time is in the hand of God and nothing is beyond his love and power. There is a union between all things and that means that each one of us is precious in every way. This small prayer asserts that the world is more mysterious than perhaps we give it credit for.

My prayer

Father, it comforts me to know that everything connects. We rely on each other. Take away one part of the chain and all fails. Let us be relaxed enough to tolerate some uncertainty and not run from the mystery of faith. Help us to see that the world and all that is in it is magical. Amen

---

PART SEVEN

For the Journey

Day 24

A Mother's Prayer

The blessing of God be to thee,
The blessing of Christ be to thee,
The blessing of the Spirit be to thee,
And to thy children,
To thee and to thy children . . .
The keeping of God upon thee in every pass,
The shielding of Christ upon thee in every path,
The bathing of spirit upon thee in every stream,
In every land and sea thou goest.

Carmina Gadelica, Prayer 292[27]

When I posted this prayer on my church website, I got quite an amazing response. Many of those who came back to me were mothers and they were feeling anxious about their children, many of whom were not at home and were out and about in a world that seemed particularly dangerous.

We never stop being parents and, even when our children are older, we still worry about them. Until the great shutdown, the world was a very mobile place. People could travel to places that their parents would never have imagined possible. But with freedom comes risk and with risk, comes worry.

This understated little prayer shows an awareness of what it's like when our children are out and about. Any mother, or parent for that matter, would surely find some comfort in the thought that Christ is shielding their children whatever path they are on. There is something very poetic about the idea that wherever our children go, in every land and sea, Jesus will be there to look after them.

Of course, one day the world and its ways will need to start up all over again. Journeys will be made; friends will be visited and the world will seem more connected than it is at the moment. But perhaps we may never feel quite at ease again and all our journeys will seem a little more dangerous than they did.

When I used to run a business, I would hop on a plane and go to all parts of the world without even thinking about it. The businesses I worked for were pretty much the same in any country that I went to. When I went to India the country was incredible, but the places I worked in were no different to the offices where I worked in Berlin, London or Paris. The world lost something of its magic. I travelled to India as though I was just popping out to the off-licence.

At this moment I've been indoors for nearly a month and the furthest anyone in my household has been is to pop over to the shop. And yet, this small journey seems fraught with risk.

I hope that when this time is over, this book will still be useful. There are always perils, and our ancient ancestors can speak to us in our times of uncertainty and difficulty. Even before our current difficulties, the terrorist attacks in London had made us think twice about travelling.

London is, of course, good at being defiant in the face of attack. My relatives went through the blitz and they carried on, just as we carried on. But after each terrorist attack I knew that I was anxious. I was anxious when my daughter travelled by public transport to places that could be a target. The comfortable business of getting on the local tube train became something that I fretted about. In these anxieties about journeys, we certainly join hands with our Celtic forebears.

The Celtic Christians celebrated journeys and asked for God's protection during them. It was a society where people mainly walked everywhere. So, there was little alternative but to appreciate the journey rather than seeing it as something that had to be got over. The destination was not the only goal and that is perhaps where we most fall. Maybe we will now appreciate journeys more and pray more often for our safety when we are on them.

The simple journey down the road to my local pub is what I miss. I enjoy the camaraderie there and watching the football and just having a simple time of relaxing. When I can go again, I think I will enjoy the journey much more than I used to.

My prayer

Father, please let us journey out without fear, knowing that you are close. Connect up our world and let us be bold citizens of the world. Be with parents as they fret about their children – especially when their children are journeying. Let us appreciate journeys again, as though they were our very first trips. Amen

---

Day 25

Our Companion

In the heart of all I greet
Love like Thine that is a grace
to homing men or roving feet.
Up the hill-way, down the glen,
Past the forest edged with broom,
Where the shadows hide the ben,
Where the rivers deepen gloom,
Radiant I, Thy lovesman go
Free from fear and safe from foe.

Hebridean Altars[28]

When I used to travel on business the worst thing about it was that I travelled alone. After a few years, however glamorous the place I was going to or staying at, I found myself just wanting to be home. Looking back on this, I think it's a bit sad, but my experience I'm sure would be shared with other people in the same situations.

It was clear to me that when we travel, it's often best not to travel alone. I wonder, though, who the perfect travelling companion would be. Would it be someone wise and funny who made us feel at ease? Perhaps it is someone with special talents and skills; a person who could help to keep us safe and know when danger was at hand.

The Celtic traveller of this prayer has a rather good journey companion. It happens to be the King of Kings and with him by his side he feels able to go from simple journeying to adventuring. It is useful if we feel lonely while on any journey to imagine the Trinity as our travelling companions. It helps us to feel less alone and to know that God is out and about with us.

Even in our high-tech world there is no place like home for most of us. We can cherish the journey and what we see and hear on it, plus we can be grateful when we can stop travelling.

My prayer

Father, we pray for all who are journeying home and all who have travelled far. We pray for companionship for the lonely traveller, and unexpected and welcome hospitality. We pray thanks for home and for the days we can stay safely with those we love. Let our journeys feel short and the people we meet be kind. Amen

---

Day 26

The Blessed Pathways

God, bless the pathway on which I go,
God, bless the earth that is beneath my sole;
Bless, O God and give to me Thy love,
O God of gods, bless my rest and my repose;
Bless, O God, and give to me Thy love,
And bless, O God of gods my repose.

Carmina Gadelica, Prayer 270[29]

After each journey, it is important that we give ourselves time to rest and recover. Journeys can be arduous, and they always take more out of us than we think they will. I wonder what the landscape was like for our Celtic brothers and sisters. I imagine that if they could time-travel, they would be completely spellbound by the way we make our journeys.

If they were plucked, say, from their homes back in the fifth or sixth century and suddenly got to see a motorway or an aircraft or a motorbike, then they would have seen it as magic – a miracle. It would be great to see them enjoying these modern wonders, especially when our own wonderment has been blunted by familiarity.

But if *we* travelled back to their time, maybe we would see something miraculous about it as well. Perhaps we would appreciate the quiet of the country and the camaraderie and fellowship of walking along the ancient paths, wishing good morning to those we met along the way. Would we have stopped along the way and taken our time to look at the Celtic standing crosses? Perhaps we would have taken a moment to enjoy the birds. But then again, the Celts might have been in just as much of a rush as we are!

This prayer shows that our Celtic ancestors were firmly rooted to the ground. It opens with a picture of a pathway and a mention of the earth beneath the sole of their foot. I cannot remember the last time I went outside without wearing my shoes, although I used to do this a lot when I was a boy. The prayer goes on to acknowledge the need for rest as well as the desire to be on the move.

When I first became a Christian in my forties, I went to a church that was established in London by South Africans. As I got to know my brothers and sisters there, I noticed some very interesting cultural differences, and these were often things I felt I could learn a lot from. One thing I noticed was the practice of praying for people if they were about to go on a journey. Those prayers were very practical and were about safety and things being well. I think I'd become so blasé about journeys that I'd stopped thinking about them other than as an inconvenience.

Jesus was often on the move, and for him, journeys were an opportunity to meet people and interact with them. If he were here now, I am sure he wouldn't be putting his headphones on and blocking out everyone around him. Dare I suggest – he might have liked a natter!

My prayer

Father, we pray as well for the pathways we travel on. Help us to travel safely and to feel the earth beneath our feet. Let the weather be good and the company jolly. Amen

---

Day 27

Staying Put

Seven times a day, as I work upon this hungry farm, I say to Thee, 'Lord why am I here? What is there here to stir my gifts to growth? What great thing can I do for others – I who am captive to this dreary toil?' And seven times a day Thou answerest, 'I cannot do without thee. Once did my Son live thy life, and by his faithfulness to show My mind, My kindness, and My truth to men. But now he has come to My side, and thou must take His place.'

Hebridean Altars[30]

What if we feel trapped where we are? What if we yearn for something more exciting? Some people would love to have the challenge of a journey and to have a fresh start. They have itchy feet. I'm very struck during this coronavirus that those with second homes frequently got in their cars and went to them because they had a choice. Others were left at home, often to do dangerous and worthwhile jobs. Some people stayed stuck and needing to do the work.

I have heard many people over the years speak about mission opportunities. There are some very exciting ones out there; and there will be again when the world begins to move. But perhaps sometimes we need to resist the call of moving and to stay put. It is just possible the greatest journey we can take is a very close one and involves journeying towards God and doing his bidding.

Perhaps the prayer is spoken by someone who is stuck in a rut; they feel that they are in a dreary place. They feel that their gifts are not being used. I'm wondering if there is some great project they could be involved in. It sounds rather like Jimmy Porter, the star of *Look Back in Anger*, who wonders if there are any good brave causes left.

The answer is both sobering and brilliant. Sometimes we are called to stay rather than to go and the journey is an internal psychological one. God gently intervenes and points out that most of Christ's life was not exactly using all of his talents. Christ didn't travel far, he stayed within a few miles of where he was born. Unlike St Paul who really did do the miles, Jesus tended to stay close to home.

God can make anything that we do into a journey if we do it for him. When we are stuck indoors, we long to be somewhere else. However, there are opportunities to serve in many ways and in many places. We don't need to use *all* our talents and we don't need to travel to a glamorous place to use them. We need to exercise our compassion towards others and do the daily business of living life well. That is a very homely journey but one that has ultimate value.

My prayer

Father, help me to be satisfied with what I have and where I am at. Help me to serve you here and now and not wonder about other places and journeys I could take. Comfort us in the mundane tasks and let us see that Christ did just the same kind of daily tasks. Amen

PART EIGHT

Hope and Trust

Day 28

The Dawn Will Come

I say to myself each night, 'The dawn will come and all that is dark be gone.' I watch the tides far ebb and whisper, 'It will flow.' In the mid of Winter, I cry to my heart, 'Soon the green banners of the Spring will blow through the land.' Yet surer still I am that Thou art my friend. For Thou hast wrought a miracle in my thought. Thou hast changed faith to knowledge and hope to sight.

Hebridean Altars[31]

One of my dear friends always used to say, 'Don't worry about anything, Sainsbury's will still be open in the mornings.' His point was that the mundane things of life will go on; the normal patterns are a comfort.

But of course, we can no longer take anything for granted. When our normality is threatened then we need to fall back on hope and trust. The Celtic Christian's thinking about hope and trust in God wasn't simplistic; it was thought through and robust. This concise paragraph is a masterclass in their way of thinking.

It begins with the kind of interior monologue that is very familiar. Each night, the speaker reassures himself that the dawn will come. It is the most basic reassurance we have – there will be a tomorrow. This is based on our experience, of course. The Celtic way is to interweave theology with story-telling. This short piece of prose does exactly that.

The subject is sitting by the fire and is becoming philosophical. He realizes that after winter comes the spring and that is a metaphor for the journey of our own lives. Of course, he puts it in the most poetic way; we have the green banners of the spring rather than just simply a single word.

Having reassured himself life always goes on, he realizes there is something even more dependable. That is that God is our friend. If we, as preachers, simply preach this message for the rest of our ministry we would not go far wrong. God is our friend. And if God is our friend then it changes the whole complexion of life. He's a friend we can trust and will always be there when we need him.

If God is truly our friend, it casts a different complexion on the way we live our lives. It re-engineers us towards hope and trust. But this friendship is not just a fuzzy feeling. It alters our minds and world-view as well. The claim is that, with God beside us, we experience being born again – utterly changed in our views, opinions and the way we see the world. This is a kind of miracle. The experience of God's kindness and closeness creates a revolution in our thought processes – and hope and trust are bound up with the way we think.

> *For Thou hast wrought a miracle in my thought. Thou hast changed faith to knowledge and hope to sight.*

I am interested in the process. Faith becomes intellectual assent – or knowledge. Faith makes sense and isn't a case of believing in the impossible or fanciful. Vague hope becomes something we can set our sight upon. We can see the end goal; we can see what is going to happen.

This reading strikes a very deep chord with me. I feel that I could almost have written it myself because it explains what happened when I became a believer in Jesus. I had been an atheist for a very long time. After a series of family disasters, we were invited to church and within a few weeks I had a conversion experience. I felt the presence of the living God and this was both exhilarating and terrifying. I was worried that it would wear off and it would just be a psychological event or state that I had gone through.

I spoke to my minister and he recommended that I read some books to explore the faith. I did a great deal more than that. I took a one-year sabbatical from my business and went to Oxford University to study Christian apologetics. It was in that year I came to see that I believed in the faith not just with my heart but also with my mind.

Heart and mind together led to the kind of revolution described in this piece. We have a sure and certain hope and that is quite different to a conditional maybe.

My prayer

Father, thank you for all the intense spiritual experience and feelings you give us. But thank you, too, that you baptize our minds as well. Help us to be confident that heart and mind confirm that you are real and are the great God of the universe. Thank you for teachers and academics and those who help us to understand theology. Amen

---

Day 29

No Nightmare Shall Lie on Me

Nor sun shall burn me,
Nor fire shall burn me,
Nor beam shall burn me,
Nor moon shall burn me.
Nightmare shall not lie on me . . .

Carmina Gadelica, Prayer 263[32]

When I was a boy, I used to suffer with night terrors. All was well during the day, but during the night I had such terrifying dreams that I began to dread going to sleep. It must have been a great worry to my parents because they were always there to reassure me and help me. I have always been a sensitive soul, with a vivid imagination.

These days, I count sleeping as one of my greatest delights and hobbies. I try to take a good rest during the day, and I like to go to bed early and wake up refreshed. Most of the time I'm fascinated by the dreams that I have. I can see that they are a way of filtering and recycling the events of the previous day. But just sometimes a dream we have is so vivid and frightening that it hangs over us for most of the day.

Much is being written about the dream life of people in a time of contagion. Newspapers report that people are having very vivid and frightening dreams. I am not surprised. When we fall under threat and under pressure our subconscious tries to work things out for us. Sigmund Freud thought dreams were the royal road to the unconscious and there is something in this. The nature of our dreams tells us something about our deepest fears and desires.

This little Celtic gem of hope and trust acknowledges that sometimes our dreams trouble us. Sometimes nightmares lie upon us like a heavy blanket and we feel we cannot wrestle free from them. But this short prayer encourages us to have hope and to know that our dreams cannot hold us captive.

Indeed, it suggests that we might be a little indestructible because our hope can conquer all kinds of fears. We do not need to fear being burned by the sun, moon or fire. We can let go of the things that are holding us down and live with a sense of freedom from fear.

But these Celtic gems also acknowledge that we are fearful people, and that is both honest and helpful. Even though we become adults, we are still in some ways the frightened child worrying about the dark. Hope can sometimes be pushed to the margins and we wonder what might happen next. Our Celtic brothers and sisters encourage us to look at fear square in the face and carry on anyway.

We are more than the sum of our nightmares. Our communities, while living through a nightmare, are finding ways to turn the darkness into light. Every time we do a good act or help another person in need, we affirm the great God of goodness. Our society and our communities are making a bold statement about human beings. We stand together against any nightmare and the darkness will not have its way.

This morning, one of my Hindu neighbours phoned to say that he will be bringing a lovely curry that he has made for us and will leave it on our doorstep. His family have done this to cheer us up and to say thank you for all the work we have done with the Memory Café here at St Cuthbert's over the years. I have missed going over to our local Indian restaurant, and so this beautiful curry will be both a tasty meal and a symbol of the great strength of our multiethnic community here in Brent. It is a brilliant place. I will eat the curry with a sense of hope and trust that God, in the end, has everything under control.

Yesterday, one of my parishioners sent me a photo of her little dog wearing a jumper. Dog and owner come to my service each Sunday, and it is a delight to have them both with us. My parishioner, Ruth, tells me that the dog knows when it is a Sunday and is waiting by the door ready to come to church. It is tiny things like this that help me to hope and trust in the people who live in these parts. Last night, I did have a very bad nightmare and this morning, as I write these words, there is something of it still in my mind. But this picture of my little dog friend has raised my spirits and helps me to know that all shall be well.

My prayer

Father, save us from the terrors of the night. Send angels to guard us and keep away terrible dreams and fears. Let us wake refreshed and full of hope for the day that lies open before us. Help us to be there to quell the fears of others with gentleness and love. Let us sleep long and softly at night all the days of our lives. Amen

Day 30

The Night Falls upon the Isles

Night falls upon the Isles. As I sit before this dying peat-fire I watch the faces of those dear ones who once lived with me in this house. Of them some now walk in the Upper Garden; others dwell in the far lands. If I moan a little, sigh a little, and say to myself – how brief a guest is joy – Thou wilt forgive. Then I remember that whether in the body or out of the body, my kin and I are members of Thy family, that one great family which is both in heaven and on earth. Then all my dark is gone.

Hebridean Altars[33]

Sometimes, my life feels as though it is full of ghosts. It's probably something to do with my age. I find myself remembering the people I no longer see and those who have moved to other countries. In these troubling times, I've also found myself thinking about the loved ones who have died. I find myself missing them, but also grateful that they don't have to go through this terrible business.

Night is falling on the island; it is a peaceful scene. There is a peat fire turning to embers and the speaker begins to think about the people who have been in his life over the years. Looking around his house, he remembers happy days and turns his mind to those who have moved far off. But even in this reverie, it strikes him that joy is fleeting and there is much to be sad about and regretted in any life.

We fear for our families and we are no different in this from our Celtic forebears. Suddenly, a cheerful and thoughtful hope enters our speaker's mind. He realizes that he and his family are part of one great family.

There is a great sense of continuity here. There are the family that we have around us and the family who have now gone to the Upper Garden, as he calls it. All are still family and still kin to the God who made the universe.

I find that hopeful.

My prayer

Father, banish my darkness and the storms within.
Send the light to banish the darkness in our lives
and communities. Let that light be a beacon of
hope and joy and a reassurance to us. Father,
St Cuthbert wrestled with the devil on the lonely
island of Farne. When we wrestle as well, be there
as our strong defender to keep the dark at bay.
Amen

Day 31

My Right Hand to my Heart

I will place my left hand to my breast,
My right hand to my heart,
I will seek the loving wisdom of Him
Abundant in grace, in broods, and in flocks.

Carmina Gadelica, Prayer 106[34]

This morning I got up early. Indeed, I have found myself waking up very early over the last few weeks. Perhaps it's a case of feeling on guard and needing to be ready to protect my family.

My normal routine is first to put the kettle on. I make a large jug of coffee and then prepare myself to face the day. We all have different routines. As a parish priest, I always try to pray in the morning and evening for my parish. Sometimes, especially on a cold and grim morning, the temptation is to stay in bed. But I resist.

I wonder if things might be better if I followed the advice in this prayer poem. Perhaps I too should place my left hand on my breast and my right hand to my heart. Then I could ask God for an infusion of his wisdom: goodness knows I need it. When I have digested this loving wisdom, I can then think on the nature of our glorious and beautiful God.

Interestingly, this tiny prayer smuggles in a useful way of understanding wisdom. Sometimes we think that wisdom is entirely something that comes from the mind. It is the passing on of knowledge and, perhaps, facts. But wisdom is much more interesting than this.

For the Celtic Christians, wisdom was about knowing things *and* being loved. Wisdom is not telling people off. Instead, true wisdom is delivered with love and comes from love. I can trust the God who is like this.

Trust in God is tied up with hope in God. We can have trust and hope because God shows himself to be loving and the source of all wisdom. When I was growing up, I was surrounded by aunts and uncles, my grandmothers and parents. We always used to have lots of my parents' friends around the house. There was nothing I liked more than sitting and listening to the stories and observations of my family and extended family. It made me hopeful that we had overcome so many things and that we were strong and true.

My prayer

Father, teach me wisdom through the stories that I hear and the love I experience. Let me always be open to learning and never stuck in rigid thought patterns. Help me to share wisdom when asked and to be quiet when not asked. Amen

PART NINE

Death and Beyond

Day 32

Jesus Accompanies Us through Death

I am going home with thee
To thy home! to thy home!
I'm going home with thee
To thy home of winter.
I am going home with thee
To thy home! to thy home!
I'm going home with thee
To thy home of autumn, of spring
and of summer.
I'm going home with thee,
Thou child of my love,
To thine eternal bed,
To thy perpetual sleep.

Carmina Gadelica, Prayer 345[35]

As a parish priest, I have the privilege of standing alongside people as they reach the end of their life. Some people seem to be calm and accepting of their situation; even joyous that the suffering they have may be close to an end. But many others fear what will happen when they die. I think that's understandable because it is one of the great unknowns of every life. We all know that one day our time will be up, but perhaps we all wonder what happens next.

We might all feel a great deal better if we read this beautiful prayer poem because it offers so much hope. It develops an interesting image and scenario. It has that crucial Celtic motif of homecoming, which is indeed the motif of this book. The Celtic Christians knew that the ultimate homecoming was the last journey to be with the gentle Christ.

In this prayer, Christ promises to go home with the person who is about to die. It says he will be with them in all the seasons of autumn, spring, summer and winter. All of us live through these seasons in our life, even those who have shorter lives than others. There is a deep seasonality about us which is something that we sometimes forget in our modern and mechanized world. The Celtic Christians knew that life goes through seasons and then at the end we die.

The image that I find most touching here is that Christ will come home with us as we reach the end. Christ affirms that each of us is his child and that he loves us infinitely. Nothing that we do can push that love away. The image of death here is one of perpetual sleep. It is a comforting image. There are many fine people working in end-of-life care, but some people towards the end of their life are burdened with isolation, illness and loneliness.

If we see death as a homecoming, that does not take away its sting, but it does help us to be not so frightened of it. If we are to be accompanied home by the King of Kings, then that takes the fear even further away.

I believe in the resurrection and the life to come. I believe that one day we will be with our friends and family and with God, living out eternity together. I believe that in that place there will be no pain or suffering and our tears will be dried. I have no problem with believing that eventually we are to return home.

If death is not the end, and after death, following a peaceful sleep, we return home to the place that will forever be welcoming, that puts a completely different slant on life. We are all heading home. Before I was a Christian, I tended to believe that when we died that was it. I found this bleak rather than liberating. It is totally in keeping with the Celtic Christian world-view that they should vividly picture life after death. After all, they had the souls of poets and so think in terms of images and metaphors.

My prayer

*Father, be with those who are near the end
of their lives. Surround them with love and
reassurance. Help us all to see that one day we
will be returning to our true home – a place of joy
where the pain of life is no more. Amen*

Day 33

Our Spirit Shall be Still

To the north the mountain ranges stood like kings upon their thrones. The sky was an arch of pearl. A cloud city, with towers and battlements complete, went floating by. The mystery of the Infinite was about us. Then the old stalker spoke. 'Is it not fine,' he mused, 'to be abroad upon a day like this? For, look you, the high places win the heart to peace, and here a man gazes on the mirror of his own eternity.'

Hebridean Altars[36]

As a vicar I seem to do many more funerals than weddings or baptisms. I'm always struck by the line 'ashes to ashes, dust to dust'. While, of course, it's true, it doesn't quite capture the great mystery of our existence. We may become dust but that's just part of the story.

In this paragraph a game-stalker is reflecting upon his surroundings. He can see the mountains and the sky. He has a poetic eye and so when he sees clouds, they become a cloud city with towers and battlements. Like many people in these situations he begins to think about mortality and immortality. Confronted with this infinite landscape and the sense that it will go on forever, where do we fit?

My father always used to say that he found rivers a bit sad. I asked him why and he told me they made him sad because he knew the river would still be flowing when he was no longer here. I wonder if this is something of the realization that this countryman is struck by.

But he isn't finished yet. He realizes that being out in the open in this extraordinary place is a very fine experience. Who wouldn't want to be in a place like this on a day like this? It fills him with peace, the kind of peace we rarely experience anywhere other than in the natural world. It's the mountains and the sky that really bring his heart to a peaceful place. He realizes that there is something of this infinity and peace within each of us. However frantic life is and difficult it can be, at the end we go to peace and peace comes to us.

Many of us have been filled with a fresh appreciation of the world around us in these difficult times. Things we took for granted in the past, we no longer take for granted. We are part of this planet and, in our death, we remain part of it. As the mountains and sky speak of infinity, we too are part of that great story.

The old deer-stalker is in a philosophical mood. Looking out into infinity prompts the question of eternity and his *own* eternity. The mountains and sky are all the sweeter with the knowledge that God made them and that he will share his company with us for all time, and even outside of time.

My prayer

Father, help us to be philosophical about life and to take time to count our blessings and ask the big questions. Let us know with certainty that the world is wonderful, and we are part of that wonder as well. Amen

---

Day 34

Comfort Me

O Holy Christ, bless me with Thy presence when my days are weary and my friends few. Bless me with Thy presence when my joy is full, lest I forget the Giver in the gift. Bless me with Thy presence when I shall make an end of living. Help me in the darkness to find the ford. And in my going comfort me with Thy promise that where Thou art there shall Thy servant be.

Hebridean Altars[37]

There is much talk these days of the need for resilience. It hints at us pulling ourselves up by our bootstraps. I have mixed feelings about it because resilience can be a stick to beat those who are feeling fragile. We have a right to be weak. Sometimes it just isn't possible to be resilient and we become broken and need fixing. But what does it take to face the future even when it is very uncertain and even when we see our loved ones becoming sick and ill around us?

This short prayer poem is packed with wisdom. The speaker begins with the need for the blessing of Christ. They point out that some days we are weary, and we feel that we have few friends. It's interesting to note that in Celtic rural settlements, where one would imagine people were never lonely, loneliness was still a fact of human existence.

The need is for the presence of Jesus and this creates joy. It also helps to correct us when we think that our successes are entirely of our own doing. But there is a deep question here about what happens at the end of our life. This prayer states that if Christ is with us at the end then we have someone to lead us home. The image that is used is that Christ will help us through the darkness to find the ford. A ford is a place of shallow water where we can cross an otherwise deeper river. In these dark times it is comforting to think that Christ will be there to lead us home.

But it doesn't end there; the prayer acknowledges that where God is, love is and we are. At the end of our time here on earth we are promised a homecoming with the greatest of hosts. That host will lead us home through the darkness over the river and into his presence. None of us like to think about death, and over the past few decades we have perhaps become insulated from it.

Each time I do a funeral at a crematorium, it occurs to me that these factories of death are kept well away from ordinary life. Out of sight and perhaps out of mind.

For the Celtic Christians, death was a daily reality. If the plague didn't get you, then something else would. But this closeness to death, and their trust in the kindly and close God, helped them to see death in a poetic, rather than totally brutal, form. I wonder if we need to rehabilitate the language of death and dying. If we live in the light of eternity and we let that guide us, are we able to see something of the promise that the Lord offers us at the end of our life?

I always feel very sorry for Lazarus. Just as he has got his dying done and prepared for the glory that awaited, Christ insisted on going and waking him up. He would have to go through it all again someday. Either way, the authorities seemed to take exception to what happened and made it look as though his second date with death might not be too far in the future. However, when Jesus meets him shortly after he has been resurrected, he has a lovely get-together and celebration. It seems that his friend has forgiven him for making him go through death all over again. At least he knows what is in store for him and in this he is one of the few human beings who have that precious realization.

I struggle very much with some of the modern humanist funerals. It isn't that I think they're wrong or they shouldn't happen. It is right that people have choice and some people feel it would just be dishonest to have a church funeral; I respect that. But I have a feeling that if you take God out of a funeral, then sometimes it seems there is not too much left. Reciting some poems and playing some favourite songs somehow does not acknowledge the brutal fact of death or offer a great deal of hope.

I wonder what our Celtic friends would make of such a funeral. I wonder too what kind of funerals they conducted.

My prayer

*Father, help us to catch some of the Celtic way
of understanding death. Help us enjoy their
metaphors and to see in them great comfort.
Father, we honour those who conduct funerals and
pray for their wellbeing as well. Amen*

Day 35

Sometimes the Gloom is Hard to Banish

The day is bright and sunny,
There is music in the meadows,
There is wine in plenty there –
That will not banish my gloom . . .
Beloved was my sweetheart,
Beauteous branch of the clustering locks,
More fragrant than cinnamon
To me the breath of thy mouth . . .

Carmina Gadelica, Prayer 551[38]

No generation takes death lightly. Even with faith in the resurrection, losing someone is hard. Dealing with other people's reactions can be difficult. Sometimes our friends avoid us because they are embarrassed about what to say.

My predominant feeling when my dad died was the brutal fact that he was no longer here, and I missed him. It was the finality that was most difficult. I remember, a few days after his death, going out into Ealing and wondering why the world was going on as though nothing had happened. It seemed incredible that the world hadn't stopped in its tracks. But my dad was just an ordinary person, a carpet-fitter and East-End boy made good and, although he was everything to us, his was an unremarkable death. I am struck that, in these awful times, the feeling of loss and the passing of ordinary but extraordinary people are all around us. For many, the world has stopped in its tracks.

We would be wrong to feel that our ancestors became desensitized to death because they saw so much of it. Or that they had such a peaceful faith that they took it all in their stride.

This lamentation gives full voice to the experience of grief and although written more than a thousand years ago it could have been written only yesterday. Here, despite the sunshine and the music and even a glass of wine or two, nothing can banish the gloom of losing the person we love. Everything has come to a halt. I guess that Jesus' followers felt just the same on the raw morning after his death.

During coronavirus, the figures for the number of people dying have been truly shocking. Each one somebody's loved one, and each one a tiny story of grief and loss.

This prayer comes from someone who has lost their partner, possibly at an early age. They still love their sweetheart and remember their physical presence. When someone dies it is the remembrance of the small details or seeing their everyday items that brings on waves of grief.

Voicing this kind of raw grief is necessary. It is touching and helps us to know that the Celtic Christians struggled just as we do when we lose someone we love.

My prayer

Father, please stand besides those who are numb with grief. Comfort those who mourn and wonder if things will ever be OK again. Stand with those who have lost loved ones and who feel bewildered and sad and perhaps angry as well. Surround those who grieve with wise friends and family who can be a comfort. Amen

PART TEN

Blessings

Day 36

The Blessing of Light

May the blessing of light be on you – light without and light within.
May the blessed sunlight shine on you like a great peat fire,
so that stranger and friend may come and warm himself at it.
And may light shine out of the two eyes of you,
like a candle set in the window of a house,
bidding the wanderer come in out of the storm.
And may the blessing of the rain be on you,
may it beat upon your spirit and wash it fair and clean,
and leave there a shining pool where the blue of Heaven shines,
and sometimes a star.

Ancient Scottish prayer,
attribution unknown

Sometimes, a piece of writing is so brilliant that it barely needs any comment. This is just such a piece. It encapsulates the very essence of the Celtic way of prayer. It is poetry and it is profound. Behind it is a clear understanding of human psychology and the bones of our faith.

Who could not be charmed by receiving the blessing of light; light without and light within? And who could not be charmed by the blessing of hospitality, friendship and good times? In times like these, this is what we miss the most.

This blessing paints a picture as a candle is set in the window of a house, bidding wanderers and strays to come in from the rain and be part of a family and to be safe at home. The Celtic Christians managed to do this kind of blessing despite living in exceptionally uncertain and difficult times. They knew that God was lived out in the ordinary lives of people and his love exhibited in the care for others that we show.

Interestingly, rain is not seen as a negative in this blessing; it is the rain that washes our spirit fair and clean and leaves a shining pool where the blue of heaven shines and sometimes a beautiful star. We live in a time of psychological rain. Indeed, if we were to paint a picture of our current times perhaps it would be belting down with rain, with thunder and storms all around us.

Before I was a Christian, I remember, one Sunday, walking with my wife along the side of the River Thames on the South Bank. It was shortly after some very difficult times, and I certainly wasn't full of the joys of spring. But walking on the path past Borough Market and with the eternal Mother Thames in sight, it certainly lifted me out of myself. I was certainly no church-goer and hadn't given God a second thought. On the off-chance, we popped into Southwark Cathedral.

A service was coming to an end and it felt peaceful, so we stayed, sitting at the back of the cathedral as observers. After the Communion, the dean invited people to come up to receive the bread and wine or a blessing. I have no idea what got into me, but I suddenly knew that I wanted – no, needed – a blessing.

I went to the front and knelt. That in itself felt significant. I suddenly felt a weight lift from my shoulders. The bishop laid a hand on my shoulder and wished me God's blessing. I cannot remember the words, but I know that I was full of lightness and felt a joy I had not experienced for months.

What was it that was going on? I wondered. It was certainly the first part of the chapter of my becoming a Christian. The act of kneeling acknowledged that there might be a more powerful force at work in the universe than I had until then believed.

But it was the business of being blessed that so moved me. It didn't feel like a magic spell. Instead, it felt like a gift. Whoever we are, we respond to the words of a blessing. Why? Because in hard times we feel beleaguered and we need to know that blessedness is at the centre of life.

As a church, we decided to put this idea of blessedness into practice. When I first came here, I think we all wondered where the church needed to go next. In the end we decided to do something both simple and profound. Our mission was to be a blessing to this community. Everything we did would bless them; no strings attached. We did it because we felt blessed by God and each other and wanted to share it around.

Blessing is a very powerful thing.

My prayer

Father, I can do no better than to repeat some of this beautiful prayer. 'And may the blessing of the rain be on you, may it beat upon your spirit and wash it fair and clean, and leave there a shining pool where the blue of Heaven shines, and sometimes a star.' Amen

---

Day 37

And More

And may the blessing of the earth be on you,
soft under your feet as you pass along the roads,
soft under you as you lie out on it, tired at the end of day;
and may it rest easy over you when, at last, you lie out under it.
May it rest so lightly over you that your soul may be out from
under it quickly; up and off and on its way to God.
And now may the Lord bless you and bless you kindly. Amen

Ancient Scottish prayer,
attribution unknown

If we accept blessing as a way of life, then it becomes a chain of joy. Where blessings score over the repeating of doctrine is that they come as a gift, and all we have to do is accept them. One of the reasons I was so influenced by the blessing I received in the cathedral was that I was amazed that it would be given to me even though I wasn't a Christian. It seemed oddly generous and I was pleased to have it.

In these angular and dangerous times, we respond to the image of the earth being soft under our feet. Yes, that really is a blessing. We respond to the empathy that comes with acknowledging that we are tired and exhausted. Rest is a blessing. I think of all the doctors and nurses and support workers who must be exhausted. They need the blessing of rest.

And there is something deeply comforting about the blessing of our last journey from life to afterlife. This is a blessing of gentle endings and good finishes.

My prayer

Father, may life lie lightly upon us. May we know your care in our dark times and bright times. May your blessing extend throughout our life here on earth and beyond. Amen

---

Day 38

In the Clasp of God's Hands

May God make safe to you each steep,
May God make open to you each pass,
May God make clear to you each road,
And may He take you in the clasp of His own two hands.

Carmina Gadelica, Prayer 277[39]

What might we ask of God if we had him here in the room with us? We probably have a whole variety of requests, but this little blessing sums up many of them.

I could pray this blessing on all those I love. If it comes to pass, it will be a great comfort to me, which is at the heart, of course, of all blessings. I would pray for my loved ones that when they're out and away from the care of this home they are made safe by God, that the doors they push will open easily and that their roads are clear.

Above all, I would want the God of gentleness and kindness to clasp his own two hands in their hands. Indeed, I long for the day when I am with God and we are able to be together and for me to hold him by the hand.

It is impossible to live life without risk. God himself took the enormous risk of being one of us. The outcome of Jesus' mission was never certain. So the divine being understands the riskiness of things on this earth.

Who could resist this blessing, especially in these troubling times? I am certainly praying it for all those who are taking a risk on our behalf. As hospitals battle to keep people alive, I pray that the doors will be open to help them get all that they need. My feeling is that we will be praying prayers of blessing for the heroes who have kept our country going in these dark times after things settle down.

My hope is that in the years to come we continue to bless them in all possible ways.

My prayer

*Father, clasp us by the hands
like the parent that you are.
Smile upon us
and let us know that
we are safe.
Amen*

Day 39

My Own Blessing

My own blessing be with you,
The blessing of God be with you,
The blessing of the saints be with you
and the peace of life eternal,
Unto the peace of life eternal.

Carmina Gadelica, Prayer 277[40]

As a parish priest, one of the highlights of my week is to preside at Communion. To welcome people to the top table of God and share in all his goodness is a great honour. Some people come up for a blessing and I always feel that this is a great testament to their faith.

This short prayer begins by the writer handing out his own blessing. As we get towards the end of this short book, I would like to hand out my blessing to you as well. This blessing is my blessing to all of you. I've been on the journey with the Celtic Christians.

For many years, I was a totally secular person; an entrepreneur, businessman; a family man. If you had told me that one day I would be a priest in the Church of England I would probably have questioned your sanity. But so it is. I have had a very blessed life, although not one without ups and downs.

To begin with the whole thing had an air of unreality. For the first few weeks after my ordination, I would walk the streets wearing my black clerical shirt and clerical collar just to get used to wearing them. These days, with God's presence, I can see that my whole life pointed in this direction. Being a priest, I'm in a strong position to pass on this blessing to you.

Standing alongside the Celtic Christians of old, I bless you and pray that the saints will be with you.

My prayer

My own blessing be with you,
The blessing of God be with you,
The blessing of the saints be with you
and the peace of life eternal,
Unto the peace of life eternal.
Amen

Last Word

I arise today, through
The strength of heaven,
The light of the sun,
The radiance of the moon,
The splendour of fire,
The speed of lightning,
The swiftness of wind,
The depth of the sea,
The stability of the earth,
The firmness of rock.

'St Patrick's Breastplate'

It has been a great pleasure for me to spend time in the company of the ancient Celtic Christians. Reading the prayers and poems and prose again has reminded me of the riches of the past. I like the way they put things because the language they use speaks of the poetry and gentleness of God.

I like their values. They value community, good times and family. They also have a strong sense; both in ordinary life and from the supernatural realm beyond.

'St Patrick's Breastplate' explains with great economy the power we have to resist disaster and feeling disconsolate. Each of us, however humble, has life and strength through the power of God. The sun and the moon, lightning and the wind and sea reassure us of God's great goodness and might. The beauty of the world we live in is a gift that we need to treasure.

St Patrick's poem is about taking on the armour of protection that is offered to us by the Trinity. We are not alone and we have friends in high places; indeed the highest place.

Our world is going to be a very different place. We will cast around for a moral compass and a new direction. Many of the things that preoccupied us before this pandemic will seem trivial and inconsequential. My hope is that something new and good may come out of it all. I hope that we will see afresh that there is no such thing as an ordinary person or an ordinary job. I hope as well that we will see that community and sacrifice are at the heart of any life well lived.

It is deeply sad and disturbing that we are seeing the deaths of a most precious generation. We have, perhaps, undervalued our elders. We have not honoured their wisdom and sense of service to their families and country. But we need them, we honour them and we pray for their safety in these very difficult times.

Who doesn't have a sense that we need protecting? Perhaps the knowledge that we need the protection of God is the first step to a widespread rediscovery of faith.

The guarding of the God of life be on you,
The guarding of the loving Christ be on you,
The guarding of the Holy Spirit be on you
Every night of your lives,
To aid you and enfold you
Each day and night of your lives.

Carmina Gadelica, Prayer 277[41]

This final prayer sums up both the Celtic Christian way, with their amazing way of doing faith, and my own journey. Before I was a Christian, I very much relied upon my own strength. In the end, though, none of us is strong enough to put up with what life has to throw at us. I learned this when I saw my father going through motor neurone disease.

When I was a boy, he was my hero. He was tough and strong and seemed indestructible. He would always stand up for me. I was a scholarly lad and not given to fighting. My dad always wanted to toughen me up because he knew how difficult life could be, but I think I may have been a lost cause. My dad, Ralph, had been a debt-collector in the East End of London and had many tough times in his life, not least losing his father towards the end of the war. I looked up to him and was awestruck by him although we had our issues when I was a teenager.

He was strong and tough, but in the end that could not help him as he lay in a hospice bed, battling with motor neurone disease. I realized then that, however tough we are, life will always throw us a curved ball. However tough Dad was, the disease was tougher – or was it? Who or what won in the end?

Even though life is very difficult at times, this beautiful prayer says that God is the strongest thing of all. In one memorable moment Jesus says that he has defeated the world. I think I know what he means by this. He means that whatever the world could throw at him, it could not in the end throw him off course. All that is worldly cannot stand up to the eternal kingdom of love and sacrifice. In the end, we put a metaphorical two fingers up at the devil and all his works.

I wish you well. Whatever life has to throw at us, we have what it takes to withstand it. The Celts knew that love will always win because it is a power that is even stronger than death.

Although they lived many, many centuries ago, we have a great number of connections with Celtic Christians. When we read their prayers and poems and prose, we feel a kinship and a sense they would understand the dilemmas and problems we face at this difficult time in our nation's life. If we were to time-travel back to the time of our Celtic forebears, many things would be unfamiliar. However, I have a strong sense that the love of hospitality and family and their appreciation of the natural world would seem very familiar to us. We would also learn a great deal from the way that they worshipped and integrated God into their everyday lives. I think we would like them, and they would like us. I certainly think that they would be full of compassion for the difficulties we are going through.

I have found that my exposure to Celtic spirituality has helped to build my own faith. As our society faces times of extraordinary change, it is comforting to look to the past and see how the people who lived there dealt with big changes as well. The Celtic Christians were a tough breed. They looked life straight in the eye and knew that nothing was certain other than God.

It seems to me that they largely had their priorities right. They had poetry in their DNA and they weren't afraid to speak lyrically and beautifully about God. During dark days we may need to discover more poetry in our own souls. The past may be another country that we choose to visit, but it is also an interesting object lesson that we do well to take note of.

This book says, 'Amen to that.'

Coming Home

One of the themes of this short book has been homecoming. In times of difficulty and anxiety, home becomes all the more important. When we come across the Celtic poems, prayers and stories, we feel a strong sense of home. As a parish priest, I know how many people rely upon the local churches for a sense of the world being safe.

As life begins to get back to normal, this sense of homeliness and family will be of crucial importance. People will feel frightened and bruised and we will need to reassure people things are going to be well. The current crisis, and other crises that may come, will change the life of our nation and the church forever. We don't know what those changes will be, but we do know that there will be changes.

Strangely, the church of the future might look a lot like the church of the distant past. The Celtic Christians tended to meet out in the open and weren't stuck inside buildings. They were full of joy and song and stories. We may find ourselves spending less time in *our* buildings and more time out and about in God's great creation.

Maybe, we will have a renewed sense of community and of gratitude for all of those who care for others. I hope that we will have even greater love and respect for elders and for all they have done and continue to do. I hope, too, that we will cherish family life and the lives of extended families as they pull together in what are sure to be difficult times.

Inhabiting the past, the world-view of our distant Christian forebears is more than archaeology. It is, instead, honouring the past in order to inform the future. Celtic Christianity has been something of an open secret for many decades. Often, people have forecast that it will influence the church and spring back into widespread acceptance. That may never happen. Celtic Christianity was always on the margins and may always be so. However, if we learn to hear the voices from the margins, we might be able to go forward in new and creative ways. I very much hope so.

In times when life seems uncertain, creativity and the arts are more important than ever. They help to remind us that we are special creatures with the ability to inhabit the world of the imagination and dream of what might be. The Celtic Christians were both very practical and dreamers and poets.

When I was at university in Norwich in the 1980s I remember one of my lecturers talking about the moon landings. He told us that NASA put together teams to try to crack very difficult problems; often scientific and very practical problems. Rather than just including scientists and engineers in these groups, they also asked poets to join. The poetic imagination added a new dimension and was exceptionally useful in helping people to ask different kinds of questions and to see life in different ways from the norm.

In many ways we face the same challenge as those NASA planners. We are about to enter into a new journey and a new reality, and we need the poets and the bards and visionaries to help us think a little more about the future.

The Celtic world is a good place to start.

Notes

1 Alexander Carmichael, *Carmina Gadelica: Hymns and Incantations* (ed. C.J. Moore; Edinburgh: Floris Books, 2006), p. 241.
2 Alistair Maclean, *Hebridean Altars: The Spirit of an Island Race* (Eugene, OR: Wipf and Stock, 2013), p. 39.
3 Carmichael, *Carmina Gadelica*, p. 60.
4 Maclean, *Hebridean Altars*, p. 7.
5 Carmichael, *Carmina Gadelica*, p. 304.
6 Carmichael, *Carmina Gadelica*, p. 63.
7 Maclean, *Hebridean Altars*, p. 25.
8 Maclean, *Hebridean Altars*, p. 18.
9 Maclean, *Hebridean Altars*, p. 16.
10 Carmichael, *Carmina Gadelica*, p. 80.
11 Carmichael, *Carmina Gadelica*, p. 299.
12 Carmichael, *Carmina Gadelica*, p. 229.
13 Carmichael, *Carmina Gadelica*, p. 93.
14 Maclean, *Hebridean Altars*, p. 92.
15 Carmichael, *Carmina Gadelica*, p. 198.
16 https://www.poetryfoundation.org/poems/45173/jubilate-agno, accessed 16 April 2020.
17 http://harvardichthus.org/about, accessed 10 April 2020.
18 Carmichael, *Carmina Gadelica*, p. 260.
19 Carmichael, *Carmina Gadelica*, pp. 127–8.
20 Maclean, *Hebridean Altars*, p. 23.
21 Carmichael, *Carmina Gadelica*, p. 179.
22 Maclean, *Hebridean Altars*, p. 6.
23 Maclean, *Hebridean Altars*, p. 101.
24 Carmichael, *Carmina Gadelica*, p. 268.
25 Maclean, *Hebridean Altars*, p. 98.
26 Carmichael, *Carmina Gadelica*, p. 187.
27 Carmichael, *Carmina Gadelica*, p. 271.
28 Maclean, *Hebridean Altars*, p. 18.
29 Carmichael, *Carmina Gadelica*, p. 244.
30 Maclean, *Hebridean Altars*, p. 22.
31 Maclean, *Hebridean Altars*, p. 108.
32 Carmichael, *Carmina Gadelica*, p. 238.
33 Maclean, *Hebridean Altars*, p. 122.
34 Carmichael, *Carmina Gadelica*, p. 109.

[35] Carmichael, *Carmina Gadelica*, p. 311.
[36] Maclean, *Hebridean Altars*, p. 42.
[37] Maclean, *Hebridean Altars*, pp. 26–7.
[38] Carmichael, *Carmina Gadelica*, p. 554.
[39] Carmichael, *Carmina Gadelica*, p. 252.
[40] Carmichael, *Carmina Gadelica*, p. 255.
[41] Carmichael, *Carmina Gadelica*, p. 255.

Lightning Source UK Ltd.
Milton Keynes UK
UKHW010843230820
368686UK00007BA/206